Mindfully Ever After

How to Stay in Love Now and Forever

Paulette Glover

BALBOA.PRESS

A DIVISION OF HAY HOUSE

Balboa Press books may be ordered through booksellers or by contacting:

Balboa Press
A Division of Hay House
1663 Liberty Drive
Bloomington, IN 47403
www.balboapress.com
844-682-1282

Because of the dynamic nature of the Internet, any web addresses or links contained in this book may have changed since publication and may no longer be valid. The views expressed in this work are solely those of the author and do not necessarily reflect the views of the publisher, and the publisher hereby disclaims any responsibility for them.

The author of this book does not dispense medical advice or prescribe the use of any technique as a form of treatment for physical, emotional, or medical problems without the advice of a physician, either directly or indirectly. The intent of the author is only to offer information of a general nature to help you in your quest for emotional and spiritual well-being. In the event you use any of the information in this book for yourself, which is your constitutional right, the author and the publisher assume no responsibility for your actions.

Cover design by Eva Montealegre
Wedding Vows by ©DJ Zelczak

Print information available on the last page.

ISBN: 978-1-9822-6442-0 (sc)
ISBN: 978-1-9822-6444-4 (hc)
ISBN: 978-1-9822-6443-7 (e)

Library of Congress Control Number: 2021903439

Balboa Press rev. date: 02/24/2021

If I had my life to live over again,
next time, I would find you sooner,
so that I could love you longer.

Unknown

Tribute to my parents, Evelyn and Ziggie. Before Ziggie left for foreign shores during World War Two, Evelyn, at seventeen years old,traveled alone by train from Pittsburgh to Kentucky so they could bemarried.

This book is dedicated with love and gratitude to
my personal angels and the light of my heart:

My son, Neil, and my daughter, Jamie,
who courageously opened their hearts to love.

My grandsons, Augie and Jude.
May you find love that lasts forever.

Wedding Vows

DJ Zelczak

I will speak of wedding vows,
The sweet promise that binds one half of
an eternal whole to its other.

Mirrored in the eyes,
Love attains a second self.

Spoken through the lips,
A song is sung of perfect love.

Heard in the air, its music heralds an eternal promise,
balanced on the pillared strength of trust and truth.

Fragrant is the air breathed in between two souls bound in
harmony and symmetry.

Gentle is the touch of a friend and a partner who pledges to forever
Be there to support, to safeguard, and to lift up the heart of love.

May God's embrace light the path of a wedded couple, and
Nurture the tree of their love, as its branches soar toward heaven for
Time everlasting.

And so I pledge to you these vows,
My life and my love.

CONTENTS

Introduction xv

PART 1
Mindfully Human

Chapter 1   Acceptance is Key..1
Chapter 2   Every Accomplishment Counts 4
Chapter 3   The Blame Game..6
Chapter 4   It's Not Personal..10
Chapter 5   The Jealousy Meter..14
Chapter 6   The Virtue of Patience..18
Chapter 7   The Heart of Being Vulnerable........................ 25

PART 2
Being Mindful

Chapter 8   Appreciation Raises Happiness Levels..................29
Chapter 9   The Season of Expectations 32
Chapter 10   The Grace of Giving and Receiving 37
Chapter 11   Living in Gratitude..39
Chapter 12   The Honor Code 44
Chapter 13   How Can I Help? 47

PART 3
Mindful Communication

Chapter 14   Respectful Communication Rocks! 51
Chapter 15   ABCs of Arguing 54
Chapter 16   Skills to Fight Right 60
Chapter 17   Listen to Hear.. 66
Chapter 18   The Sounds of Silence..70
Chapter 19   Embracing a Safe Environment.......................... 73

Chapter 20   Sulking Is For Kids..75
Chapter 21   "I" Statement Communication............................ 79

PART 4
Mindful Infrastructure

Chapter 22   Forgiveness Is Freedom 85
Chapter 23   Infidelity Hurts 90
Chapter 24   In-Laws Are Not Outlaws 93
Chapter 25   Respect Is the Golden Rule of Marriage.................... 98
Chapter 26   Trust in Love 101

PART 5
Mindful Money

Chapter 27   Finances Take Compromise 105
Chapter 28   Final Wishes Are Forever 109
Chapter 29   The Savings Plan 112
Chapter 30   Teamwork Gets the Job Done 117

PART 6
Mindful Living

Chapter 31   Atmosphere Sets the Vibrational Tone 123
Chapter 32   Eat, Rest, and Be Merry 126
Chapter 33   Who's the Boss?..128
Chapter 34   Hugs Are Free... 131
Chapter 35   Lucky in Love 133

PART 7
Mindful Romance

Chapter 36   Flirting Is a Silent Tango 139
Chapter 37   I Love You More 141

Chapter 38   Kissing Is More Than a Kiss........................... 143
Chapter 39   Wellness Pampering Is a Gift of Love......................... 145
Chapter 40   Be Playful and Touch the Sky........................ 147
Chapter 41   A Sense of Humor Uplifts the Spirit............................ 149
Chapter 42   Does Sex Really Matter?.................................... 152
Chapter 43   Sexy Is as Sexy Does 155
Chapter 44   Words to Love By 158

PART 8
Mindfully in the Now

Chapter 45   Forever Friends 165
Chapter 46   Rejuvenate! 167
Chapter 47   Interests 169
Chapter 48   To Sleep or Not to Sleep?.............................. 171
Chapter 49   Space in Your Togetherness 175

PART 9
Mindful Beliefs

Chapter 50   Where Faith Resides...............................181
Chapter 51   The Circle of Love 184
Chapter 52   The Will to Love 186

Gratitudes... 191
References 197

INTRODUCTION

My hand naturally glided into his as though it had been there before—warm, snug, comfortable. My future husband guided me to the dance floor with ease, somehow knowing our bodies would fit together like yin and yang. Corny as it sounds, I felt like Cinderella meeting my Prince Charming. When the music stopped playing at the stroke of midnight, neither one of us wanted to say good night. So, unlike Cinderella who dashed away to her awaiting pumpkin, I agreed to venture onto his cousin's well-worn pontoon boat, and within the hour we were leisurely puttering into the pitch blackness of the Monongahela River.

It wasn't until we were in the middle of the river that my prince realized his cousin had neglected to tell him that one of the pontoons had a major leak. Not that it would have mattered. As the boat's exaggerated tilt sank deeper into the murky waters, we talked until dawn.

A mere year after our meeting, we had the word *forever* engraved inside thin wedding bands that would be paid off in just twelve easy installments. We didn't care that he had another year of college and I had my first teaching job at a salary of a whopping five thousand dollars a year. What we didn't have in money was made up for with fiery chemistry that could split an atom.

Convinced our love would conquer all, we called our parents the morning we planned to elope. This was by no means a spontaneous decision. We had previously found a little church in Maryland where there was a kind minister who spoke with us about love, commitment, and the sanctity of marriage. We talked about the future and how we would be one of those old couples who always hold hands, finish each other's sentences, and call each other "Mom" and "Dad."

In truth, we had no idea what we were doing. Time proved that love wasn't enough. Through the years, outside factors and meddlesome people cunningly seeped into our lives, playing manipulative games under the guise of caring. The future of our marriage was doomed; we just didn't know it. Just as I had ignored the sinking pontoon, it took me twenty-three years to take responsibility for the underlying feelings of lies and deceit that came to define our marriage.

By the time we sought counseling, the relationship was far too fractured to be repaired. The gray, dingy clouds aptly predicted what was to come that fateful day as we walked up the steps of the therapist's office building. I, for one, had high hopes that he could save us. During that one-hour meeting, we first met with the psychologist together, then individually, then together again. At the second together meeting, the doctor told us that he needed to see my husband by himself. He said that *his* issues had to be dealt with before he could help us as a couple.

With a brief sense of relief that my suspicions were confirmed, I felt a deep sigh release the tension I had been holding firmly within my body. But as I recovered, I realized that there was no real cause to celebrate. I felt the counselor's gaze through his thick, black-rimmed glasses. His smile was gone. Neither did he give us any word of encouragement. Not one word. His solemn tone told me that we weren't fixable. My glance moved to my husband as I searched for a sign of hope, but he was mindlessly staring into space. The man I shared my life with couldn't even look at me. Intuitively, I knew we were over. It was a very quiet ride home.

For the longest time, being divorced bothered me. The word stuck in my throat like a frog that couldn't hop. The first time I had to check "single" on my tax return made me physically ill. Divorce shouldn't happen to any couple as much in love as we had been. Not to us. Yet, it did.

Granted, I've been told that I look at the world through rose-colored glasses, and while I readily admit that I have a tendency to be gullible and naive, the one thing I had learned was the value of discernment, the necessity of setting boundaries, and to seek help sooner rather than later. So when I married again eight years later, and a boundary was broken, I offered him a choice—therapist or attorney. He chose the attorney.

While I never imagined I would be writing the intimate details of my personal life for all the world to see, I'm grateful to be able to share the lessons I have learned and for the spiritual guidance that led me to know that I'm exactly where I'm meant to be. What began with an idea, a yellow tablet, and determined desire to help couples honor love, this guide developed to prevent and identify problems *before* they reach the point of no return.

There are many mindfully ever after marriages and yours is most likely one of them. By becoming aware of the snags and snares ahead of time, you're certain to gain sure-footed confidence on how to keep the sanctity of the vows you made to one another.

The challenge for couples is blending embedded tribal beliefs, desires, and expectations to create the ideal marriage. Although there's no one-size-fits-all set of rules for everyone, reading this book offers the opportunity for meaningful discussion. Matrimony requires supernatural vigilance to recognize seemingly insignificant issues, prevent them from escalating, and reach resolution before they become a volcanic mountain of irresolvable differences. If you take the same tender care a winemaker exerts as he watches over his vineyard, your love is destined to mature to a ripe old age.

Naturally you're going to have differences of opinions. There will be changes in job situations. And, people will float in and out of your lives who prove to be influential challenges. You may even have a strained living arrangement. Know that whatever has happened to you has happened to someone else. Pay attention and learn from others! You are not alone. By keeping your values and goals intact, you're certain to stand in truth with one another for now and always.

Although there are no guarantees in life, living in the zone of mindfulness is truly a pathway to a loving, calm, and caring tomorrow for an ever-after lifetime of happiness. Thank you for taking Mindfully Ever After on your magnificent journey of love. I applaud your commitment.

As you embark on this incredible adventure, I wish you Godspeed. Just as the astronauts did when they rocketed to the moon, as you cross the threshold to a life together, strap in for the ride of your life!

Love is energy.

Love connects your heart with your spirit with a vibration frequency of 528 Hz. (Jankowiak 2014)

Love's vibration is the same as Earth's vibration.

Tune to the frequency of love.

PART 1

Mindfully Human

Human beings have a highly developed brain, the aptitude for articulate speech, and the ability of abstract reasoning. One of the greatest gifts of being human is acquiring wisdom from family stories and passing them on from generation to generation, including pearls like when great Grandma was asked to reveal her secret to living to one hundred, she said "Hell if I know! I just open my eyes every morning and I'm still here!"

The other great thing about being human is that we possess hands! With hands, you can give a gentle pat to the tush, hold your love's face while saying "I love you," caress the hills and valleys of your love's body and explore every nook and cranny. Holding hands, sharing foot massages and back rubs are a few of the ways humans bond in the rituals of expressing love.

Human beings are intricate, amazing creatures full of creativity, capable of compassion and love and a sense of hope and adventure. While possessing all of those wonderful qualities, humans are also influenced by genes, environment, cultural attitudes, and personal preferences. Along with an assortment of tribal, religious, and political beliefs of ancestors who have long since passed, some may even maintain that where the astrological stars are in alignment when birth occurs has a major influence over an individual's life choices and potential.

Yet, wonderful as we are, humans are flawed. Humans make mistakes. Of course, not you—you're perfect! But many typical humans, even those who have the intellect to cure diseases, who have thumbs to button a shirt, and who can read magazine articles full of knowledge to guarantee happiness are often not content with their chosen partner.

Have you ever found yourself on the hamster wheel of repeating choices that lead to the same consequences, and then, in innocence, wonder why? It's crucial to recognize the history of patterns of behaviors in order to make positive changes in your life. While some people learn quickly and move on with great success, there are others who seem to be doomed to repeat life lessons. To end the negative cycles affecting relationships, overall health, and mental well-being, be aware of your actions of the past and mindful of your thoughts of today.

One thing is for certain, where there is the hope of love, humans will find a way.

CHAPTER 1

———— ❖•❖ ————

Acceptance is Key

*Accept all of your partner's quirks,
habits, and little annoyances.*

HUMANS ADOPT LITTLE QUIRKS AT an early age, some more annoying than others, like shuffling feet or cracking gum. Sharing your life with a partner who accepts all the little quirks you've gained along the way paves a natural path to a harmonious home.

Once chemistry clicks on the first date, all of your attention is focused on getting to know each other. You may learn that he collects stamps and loves to travel. You find out that her idea of camping in the great outdoors means staying at a lodge. At this level of dating, she doesn't know if he leaves sweaty socks on the living room floor, hoards newspapers, or drinks milk from the carton. He doesn't know if she farts in bed or dulls his razor by shaving her legs. These are things couples usually learn after a commitment has been made.

Months or years later, the quirks that weren't much of a bother at the early stages of romance may become maddening! Some habits are easier to fix than others, like sticking gentle reminders on the bathroom mirror: "Clean out the sink, damn it!"

Having trouble changing your annoyance level? Instead of homing in on what drives you crazy, switch to the energy channel RIPT: recognize individual positive traits.

Jamie said, "Adam and I respect each other and can talk openly about anything. Even more than that, we totally accept each other. For example, when Adam's working on a project, he's so laser focused that he doesn't hear a word I say. I've learned to accept that's who he is and wait to talk to him after he's done. When I'm moody or not feeling up to par, Adam accepts me. I don't try to change him, and he doesn't try to change me."

Granted, there are definitely behaviors that go beyond being annoying that are not acceptable.[1] These habits often have to do with smelly bodily functions or personal cleanliness, like crawling into bed with dirty feet or neglecting oral hygiene. Basically, consistent neglect of personal hygiene points to a more serious problem.

Be aware of your misperceptions of marriage. Honeymoons really do come to an end, couples really are two individuals with separate thoughts, and getting married really isn't the end-all answer to solving personal problems. Marriage is about accepting the warts along with the halos.

After forty-one years, Walter succinctly summarized: "You must be respectful friends. Love each other, accept the differences, and don't

---

[1] Quirks and habits are not traits like lewd behaviors, an interest in porn, physical/emotional abuse, deceit, or abuse of alcohol or drugs. These behaviors may require professional assistance.

get stuck on issues. Things are just what they are, not always to be changed to suit someone else. The time that you spend convincing someone to think as you do can be futile and frustrating. Life goes on anyway, and every small issue usually wanes in importance the next day. I guess what I'm saying is, just accept each other, the good along with the not so good. It all levels out in the end."

By accepting each other's minor quirks and habits, you remain one solid unit. Change what's necessary, accept the little annoyances, and, please God, grant the wisdom and ability to know the difference.

CHAPTER 2

Every Accomplishment Counts

Offer sincere praise for your partner's
accomplishments. Big or small,
each accomplishment benefits your togetherness.

AS A NEW BRIDE, I wasn't much of a cook. Oh, I conquered the scrambled egg well enough, but the challenge of making lump-free mashed potatoes and gravy escaped my kitchen prowess. It all came out too thick, too thin, or too lumpy. I used too much flour, too little broth, too much salt, not enough butter. Until one fantastic Thanksgiving, I made the absolute best mashed potatoes and gravy ever made on that thankful day! It was like the fairy godmother of lump-free food waved her magic wand, and I could do no wrong.

When my husband told me how delicious everything was and how proud he was of me for never giving up, I was like a little kid! "Watch me swim!" "Watch me swing!" "Watch me make gravy!" It's embarrassing to admit, but I remember telling him every single step of the mashed-potato-and-gravy process and how I had accomplished it!

Human nature is a funny thing when egos come into play. Of course, egos are necessary, but when it comes to accomplishments, it's time to set your own ego aside and let your partner shine. Love is about having the genuine satisfaction that you offered unwavering support and had faith in her every step of the way.

Be careful, however. An accomplishment by one partner can quickly become a two-edged sword if you let your ego get the best of you. In other words, don't let your fifteen minutes of fame go to your head, or, as my mom would say to my brothers and me: "Don't get too big for your britches, missy!" or "Don't get too big for your britches, mister." Clearly, anyone approaching big-britches status wasn't worthy to be called by name. When she felt that enough praise had been given, another favorite saying was, "It's time to come off that high horse of yours." Which was especially interesting, as none of us—including her—had ever ridden a horse. So, while you have every right to be proud of your accomplishments, remember the people who helped along the way. If you don't, beware of losing your britches or falling off of that horse.

Be proud of each other's accomplishments, whether it's a promotion at work, earning an advanced degree, or hanging a picture. Recognize with pride the dedication of all the hard work and sacrifice your loved one has made.

Meanwhile, if you're the one receiving recognition, don't let your ego get the best of you. Arrogance and bragging do *not* paint a pretty picture. Acknowledge the support your partner gave along the way to make your accomplishment possible. In the long run, every accomplishment benefits the home team.

CHAPTER 3

The Blame Game

Stop playing the blame game.
Take responsibility for your own actions.
Recognize when blame is unfairly placed.
ARM yourself:
Accept the situation with grace.
Release anger by seeking a solution.
Move on with resolution.

"WHO KNOCKED THE PLANT OVER?" Mom asks. All the kids chime in at once, pointing at each other, "It's his fault!" "She did it!" "Not me!" Finger pointing and blame are usually assigned to the young.

While most people grow out of the blame game, some carry it into adulthood, placing blame for any missteps in daily life: "It's your fault I missed my meeting." "You made me miss my exit." "Why did you let the dog chew my shoe?" "Why didn't you tell me it was my mother's birthday?" With people who are in the habit of constantly placing blame, the list is endless.

To be fair, abuse of the blame game is gender equal, with both sexes causing havoc on the spirit. By the time you're an adult, it's time to act like one by taking ownership of your decisions and behaviors. Stop being defensive and accept that placing blame is childish and does nothing to serve any relationship's best interest.

When I was a kid, my family's running joke was to blame the dog anytime anyone had flatulence. Boots would hear her name, lift up her head, and look at us fools laughing, as though saying, "Whatever." While your dog doesn't care, I guarantee that, if you're constantly blaming your partner, he or she does care. As time goes on, a once-confident mate can become filled with embarrassment, fear, or anger. Without understanding why, your partner may become anxious or withdrawn as the body internalizes the resentment, pain, and shame.

How mindful are you about placing blame? Are you self-aware enough to take ownership of your actions and words? Is your partner often saying, "I'm sorry"? Everyone makes mistakes; that's part of being human. If you leave the closet door open and the dog chews your shoes, is it fair to blame your partner for not watching the dog? If you're the one driving and not paying attention, who's responsible as you speed past the exit? If your mother's birthday is coming up, who is responsible to remember it?

If you have an honest desire to recognize and release the toxic patterns of placing blame, the time to take responsibility is *now*. By making a mindful shift of your perception when things don't go the way you expect, compassion and understanding will gratefully replace the pointed finger of blame.

Once empathy takes the place of finding fault, simply by putting yourself in the other person's shoes, you'll gain a shift in conscious awareness of what's really happening. Start by answering questions: Why didn't you take the time to close the closet door to protect your shoes? Why weren't you watchful of the exit? If you knew that the car needed gas, why didn't you get it the night before or leave a little earlier? Instead of placing blame, discuss a common-sense solution. By being mindful of your *own* actions, the blame game can be a thing of the past.

Realize that placing blame is not the same as calling someone out on consistent, unhealthy habits or annoying behaviors. For example, the one outstanding complaint I heard regarding placing blame was the lack of time management. In other words, one partner was always late to events, movies, dinner reservations, etc. Regardless of excuses, the act of constantly being late would often end in a futile argument without changes in behavior.

If this is one of your complaints, a few preventative solutions may improve time management skills. One solution is as simple as setting a bunch of cell phone alarms as reminders to stay on track. Another technique is the clever use of notes. When stuck to the computer screen, the bathroom mirror, bedroom dresser, or even the coffee pot, these quiet reminders raise awareness to stay on track. Notes to yourself also serve as silent prompts on the car steering wheel when you need to pick up a kid from soccer practice. You could even try the old-fashioned method of tying a string around your finger to remember to buy milk. One woman used the sticky note app on her computer to compose her things-to-do list. Yet another got an hourglass timer to keep her on track. Where there's a will, there's a way.

Once ownership of any chronic problem is accepted, along with a sincere willingness to correct it, relationships improve. Gratitude replaces nagging. Patience replaces anger. Then, if you're late to a major event, it's because you honestly did get delayed in traffic.

When a habitual problem is first mentioned, your partner may feel insulted or angry and become defensive. While not everyone is compliant, once the problem is out in the open, your relationship may actually be strengthened because no one is seething in resentment or harboring the feeling of being taken for granted.

Be honest with yourself. Rather than seeking fault or placing blame, search for ways to resolve the issue. Professional help may be able to uncover the root of the problem and offer a simple solution, leaving you saying, "Why didn't we think of that!"

> **A**ccept with grace that there is a problem.
> **R**elease your anger by seeking a solution
> **M**ove on with resolution.
>
> ARM yourself—Accept. Release. Move on.

CHAPTER 4

———·❧·❧·———

It's Not Personal

*Be mindful of the perceptions you make
about the people around you.
Adopt the "it's not personal" attitude
for inner peace and contentment.*

WHATEVER IS SAID OR DONE, whether by your partner, a parent, a boss, or a stranger in passing, know that it's not personal! I know the internal struggle it takes not to personally accept insults when they seem directly aimed at your heart. But know that, when you do take other people's words or actions personally, you're giving them power over you while they merrily row along in their boats, whistling a happy tune, leaving you feeling like a piece of lint flicked off a sleeve.

By simply changing your perception of any person, place, circumstance, or event, you can cause an entirely new scene to open up to you. Look through the windshield of your car. What you see is what you get. It isn't personal that there are construction delays, detours, and potholes.

Even if a person's dog craps in your yard, it isn't personal. Maybe he forgot to bring a cleanup bag, or he's just plain rude. Accept that there will always be rough roads, changing scenery, and people who let their dogs crap in your yard. It's all part of the human experience. Accept that there are rude and ignorant people regardless of where you live. Also know that there are more kind and thoughtful people if you permit yourself to *see* them through a compassionate lens. When you don't take on other people's baggage, your thoughts are open to new ideas.

Once upon a time, I was promised a supervisor position if I returned to grad school for certification, which I did. Thousands of dollars in debt later, when the position became available, it was given to someone else. Was I upset? Hell, yeah. Did I take it personally? Oh, yeah. At the time, my perception was skewed with personal doubt. What I didn't realize was that the Universe had other plans for me.

I don't know why things happen the way that they do, but I have come to realize that, when you don't take things personally, the Universe may be giving you a nudge to find the opening to your true path. Hurts and disappointments are bound to happen, but once you refuse to have your emotions dictated by other people, you're able to surrender and open yourself to be more discerning when new opportunities come your way. What you *want* and what you *need* are two different things for personal growth.

Look at the people in your life. You are in contact with kind people, open-minded people, selfish people, and judgmental people in your everyday life. It's your choice to be with people who offer kindness and respect. Walk away from people who exude toxic energy. Once you stop taking the negative actions of others personally, you'll find your relationship at home becomes less stressful and more satisfying. It's impossible to please everyone, so you must have the courage to be true to the one person who matters most—yourself. For myself, on the exact evening of the day that I found out that I didn't get the promised position, an unexpected and totally different path opened up that led me on the incredible spiritual journey that has culminated in this book.

Know that there will be people in your circle of friends or immediate family who won't understand when you no longer give permission to have your buttons pushed. After all, you've stopped playing the game. When you hear, "My, how you've changed!" and you're able to respond, "Thank you for noticing," feel the pride of taking control of your life.

A Mindfulness Story about a Man, a Hole, and Changing Negative Patterns

A man walked down the street one day and fell into a hole.

The next day, he walked down the same street and again fell into the same hole.

On the third day, he remembered the hole, but he was daydreaming and not paying attention, so he fell into the hole a third time.

On the fourth day, he remembered the hole and was mindful to walk around it.

On the fifth day, he took complete control and walked down a different street where there were no holes.

Be mindful of patterns you've established in your life and know when it's time for you to walk down a different street.

Trust your inner voice. By integrating "it's not personal" as your guided truth, you gain inner peace and happiness, regardless of the bumps in the road. You'll be able to accept them for what they are— just bumps.

A Simple Story of "Empty Boats"

There was once a man who dearly loved his boat. Every day, he cleaned and polished it to a mirror glaze. No one in his family was allowed to touch it. Once a week, he would take his precious boat onto the lake by himself.

One day, as he reached the middle of the lake, a light mist moved in. He could faintly see a boat coming directly toward him. He screamed, shouted, and wildly waved his arms! "Stop! Watch out!" But soon he felt a hard *thud*! His precious boat had been hit! As he ran his hand over the dent, his anger grew. He yelled and cursed until veins popped out of his neck. "Why didn't you watch where you were going! What's the matter with you?" On and on.

No one replied, and as the mist lifted, he could see he had run into an old abandoned boat that was drifting aimlessly.

The realization hit him. He had been blaming a person in the other boat for his anger, but there was no other person. The boat was empty. The man realized that the anger was within him and him alone. It had been within him all along.

The point is, if the boat is empty, there is no one to be angry with, even though your boat still received the bump. It is what it is. And nothing more.

It may take years to fully integrate the "it's not personal" philosophy, but once you do, it's an exhilarating experience to be liberated from other people's negative energies. Every once in a while, I catch myself sliding, and I have to be mindful that the behavior of the other person has nothing to do with me. Whatever happens, whatever is said, it isn't personal. Know that you are enough just the way you are. Be mindful of the empty boats in your life and search inward for answers.

CHAPTER 5

·❦·

The Jealousy Meter

Keep your jealousy meter in check.
Healthy jealousy adds romantic zest and zing.
Irrational jealousy is destructive and leads to disaster.

IMAGINE GOLDILOCKS PUTTING SUGAR IN her coffee the next time your jealousy alarm is triggered: Too little leaves a bitter taste and too much makes it undrinkable. When it comes to jealousy, you need to find the amount that's "just right." If you aren't the jealous type, your partner may feel you don't care. If you're too jealous, your partner could feel suffocated and be driven away. The "just right" amount of jealousy is a delicate balance.

What *is* the precise amount of acceptable jealousy? Imagine that you and your partner are in a crowded room at a well-attended party. You happen to glance over and notice that a particularly attractive person is getting a little too chummy with your significant other. The hair on the back of your neck stands at attention with jealousy. As you watch the interaction, look at your innocent partner from a new angle—you can certainly understand why someone would want to get to know him or her better. A realization washes over you. Your partner is kind of cute and definitely witty. No wonder others pay attention. But you're the one with the ring on your finger. You're the one going home to make love.

To let your spouse know that you know how hot you think he is, casually walk over, lock your arm through his, and look the "flirter" in the eye, smile, offer an extra squeeze to your spouse's arm, and say, "This one belongs to me" or "I see you've met my other half." This gentle show of healthy jealousy can stimulate your passion for each other, and it could last for weeks. Your partner feels desired, and you're reminded what a great catch you have. Mild jealousy may even add a little zest and zing to your marriage and intimacy.

On the other hand, visualize the same party, but this time, imagine that your jealousy gets the best of you. You do nothing at the gathering, but your ears puff steam like a whistling teakettle. On the way home, you make a number of irrational accusations. In bed, you turn your back to him, blaming him for the attention of the flirter. With this level of jealousy, at the next party, your partner will be afraid to talk to anyone for fear of facing your wrath. He will become uncomfortable in social situations and eventually prefer to stay home where he can't be accused of doing anything wrong. An overly jealous mate kills the flame and needs to examine his or her own thoughts, beliefs, and perceptions. Was Clark Kent jealous when Lois Lane loved Superman?

Imagine the one-eyed Cyclops or the flying Pegasus. Just because you can picture them in your mind's eye, doesn't make them real. The same goes with jealousy. Frequent or irrational jealousy can be a sign of insecurity and can do long-term damage to any relationship. To check your jealousy meter, ask, "Do I want to spark a cozy campfire? Or, do I have an unconscious need to toss away all I hold dear into a raging bonfire?" Mild and occasional jealousy is common in any healthy relationship. Do yourself a favor and leave the overactive imagination to the moviemakers.

What about being jealous of your spouse's career? This is harder to deal with simply because being jealous of your partner's success kind of makes you look like a jerk. Technically, by criticizing or making unkind innuendoes about the success of your other half, you're shooting yourself in the foot. So, if you feel the pangs of insecurity or envy at your partner's achievements, open your heart to admiration and support, knowing that couples who complement each other are forever. Appreciate that the success of one benefits both.

Aline recalls that for her and David, "It really was love at first sight. I just knew that David was the one for me. It was his eyes! We married within the year." Her eyes glistened as she reminisced about the complete trust they shared in their marriage. While David traveled extensively with his job, Aline pursued her passion for art by studying with well-known artist, Henry Koerner. Wherever David and Aline went, whomever they saw, or whatever the circumstance, there was never any room for jealousy.

"David was very good looking, and women would flirt with him, but I wasn't concerned. I always knew he was mine. I would think, *Wow! She likes him, too. Go ahead and flirt with him!* I knew that was as far as it would go. He trusted me too. When I was teaching or studying art with Henry, I would be out late at night, and David never once questioned me. We made a commitment and were very much in love. David had incredible integrity in every aspect of his life. That was why everyone, including me, trusted him so completely and why he had the reputation of being "solid." We shared the same family values too. We were made for each other. I was very lucky."

Aline and David shared forty-five years with faith and trust in their love. "When David became ill, that trust brought us closer than ever.

We knew that we would always be there for better or worse, no matter what happened, to the very end of our lives here on earth."

My Dad's Lesson about Jealousy

The next time you're at the beach or near a playground sandbox, pick up a handful of sand and loosely open your hand.

Notice how the sand peacefully rests free of movement in the palm of your hand, with no intention of leaving.

Now, take another handful of sand and make a tightened fist. Watch as the sand slides through your fingers.

So it is with jealousy.

CHAPTER 6

―――――・❧・❧・―――――

The Virtue of Patience

*Cultivate patience by releasing your fairy tale notions of
love and marriage.
Breathe deeply, stay positive,
and be patient with yourself and others.*

"BE PATIENT. GOD ISN'T FINISHED with me yet." This saying is a gentle reminder to honor the reality that humans are constantly learning and growing.

Today's culture is one of instant gratification. The virtue of patience plays a constant tug of war with the weakness of impatience. While I'm grateful that technology has made it possible to access an encyclopedia's worth of information with one tap of the finger, I wonder if that same technology has spoiled people and made them less patient with one another.

Remember when your parents would tell you to count to ten before getting "angry" when your sibling smeared lipstick over your Beatles poster or stuck a frog in your purse? Well, it turns out that taking deep breaths actually does help with learning patience. The following three exercises are beneficial to learning patience.

Exercise 1: Deep Breathing and Affirmations

Deep breathing plus positive affirmations are helpful techniques for teaching the subconscious mind what it means to be patient. Keep in mind that the subconscious is like a head of cabbage. It isn't capable of knowing the difference between the truth and a lie. Over time, the brain can be rewired to think differently about the world. As you say positive affirmations with high-frequency confidence, you replace low-frequency or negative vibrations, like making judgments about yourself or others. Eventually, the brain starts processing a more constructive outlook on life. So if you truly aspire to bring more patience and peace into your being, the following exercise practiced daily will help. Affirmations change negative thoughts into positive ones for health, wealth, relationships, spiritual growth, and any topic of concern.

Mindfulness and breath awareness go hand in hand. To begin deep breathing, sit comfortably with your spine erect and feet on the floor. Sitting in this way aids in the flow of energy and keeps the body grounded. Keep your palms open, resting them gently on your lap Do *not* cross your legs, ankles, or arms; that can block the flow of energy. There is no need for any fancy sitting position, like lotus style or with fingers touching, called a mudra. Locate a comfortable and quiet space, where you can be alone and undisturbed, open to receive the calming energy flow throughout your body. This isn't hocus-pocus. It's just one technique to add to your basket of tools that can help you gain awareness of your subconscious mind through breathing.

Now close your eyes and begin your deep breathing. Focus on being aware only of your breath. Take a deep breath and close your eyes. Slowly, exhale. Relax. When distracting thoughts come to you, no matter what they are, silently acknowledge each one and tell it that you'll get to it later. After releasing the thought, return to the awareness of your breath. Take another deep breath and again, slowly release your breath. After all the air has been released, hold it for a few seconds before taking another deep breath. As you breathe, recite your affirmations aloud or to yourself. Pick one of my suggestions, or several that are relevant to your current situation. Or make up your own—whatever feels right.

Feel the lightness as the stress of the day is replaced with positive affirmations. When you finish breathing your affirmations, place your hands on your heart to lock in the tranquil feeling of being in control. Then slowly open your eyes. Don't be in a hurry or force the process. Let the positive energy integrate into your being. Listening to soft music or to a guided meditation may also encourage a tranquil feeling as the energy streams throughout your body. Ready, set, breathe:

Every day is the best day.

I am calm.

I love myself.

I am patient.

I am the best I can be.

I am strong.

I am enough.

I am happy.

I am creating the perfect day.

I am healthy.

I am patient with myself and others.

I am relaxed.

While breathing, close your eyes and picture yourself in your mind's eye being calm and relaxed. Different people, places, circumstances and events may float in and out as you release any negative thoughts. Your body may heave a sigh as stress is being released. Repeat your affirmations daily until you feel confident that you've integrated the positive thoughts into your subconscious mind. Be patient with yourself. As your mindfulness grows through meditation, so will you manifest a feeling of inner calm by taking conscious control of your decision making.

Exercise 2: Self-Introspection

This exercise helps with self-introspection. Again, sit comfortably with a straight back, feet on the floor, and open hands resting on your lap. Now inhale through the nose to the count of seven. Hold the breath to the count of seven. Exhale to the count of seven. Hold the breath to the count of seven. Do this round of breathing seven times, sending vital energy to the cells. As you exhale, imagine yourself blowing out stress and negativity. If you find the count of seven difficult, start with a count of four and work your way up.

This process helps you to find inner calmness and reduce stress by releasing the chatter of the monkey mind.

Exercise 3: Pep Talk

Stay positive by repeating your affirmations in front of a mirror. Visualize yourself being calm and peaceful until it becomes integrated into the subconscious as part of your belief system. The more you release judgments of yourself and others by deleting negative thoughts that serve you no purpose, the sooner your subconscious will learn to react with calm in place of irritation. This transmutation takes time, so don't give up—It *will* happen. During your mirror talk, speak as though you're giving a pep talk to a friend. Be a friend to yourself. Encourage yourself. Believe in yourself.

The subconscious is where your memories, fears, and beliefs are stored. It asks no questions as it directs the pattern of your thoughts, hopes and desires. That knowledge is strengthened by the emotion attached to it, so whatever you *truly aspire* becomes imbedded into the subconscious mind and then manifests into reality. Wherever you direct your emotion, energy follows. Remember: emotion directs energy.

Retraining the subconscious mind to release negative thoughts is like planting seeds. With fertile soil, clean water, and plenty of sunshine, it's possible to see positive growth in as little as a few weeks. By consistently practicing patience early in your marriage, you are better equipped to transform fairy tale beliefs into years of forever-after love.

Above all else, be patient with yourself. The duckling doesn't turn into a swan overnight.

Julie says, "Derek and I've been married thirty-one years. We started dating when we were teenagers. For us, making our marriage work is a combination of things. Patience is most important. And being considerate of each other is huge! It really is the little things that matter. No matter what happens, we remember to be patient with each other." She adds, "He's my best friend, so it's easy."

A Lesson from My Dad in the Late 1950s

We were watching a variety television program when I made an unkind comment about a man playing an instrument. I said he was ugly.

My dad asked me to repeat my comment. Reluctantly, I repeated what I had said, including the word *ugly*. He then asked if I thought that he was ugly.

"Oh no!" I assured him. "You're very handsome!" In my adoring eyes, he was the handsomest of men.

"You think so? Well, do you think, if that man has children, they would think he's ugly?"

"I don't know." I said, feeling ashamed, knowing that a lesson was about to come.

He said, "I want you to understand that God made each and every one of us. We don't have any control over how we look. But we do have control over our actions. People who are mean, hurtful, or have a temper *act* ugly. How we look is never ugly. It's what's inside, what you can't see, that is important. If we live lives of integrity, if we are honest and kind—now, that's a beautiful person.

This man on TV is offering us music. So, instead of commenting on how he looks, see and hear the gift he's giving for us to enjoy. Remember, it's not the outside wrappings, it's how the person is on the inside that matters."

Ever since that day, I have *never, ever* again used the word *ugly* to describe a person's appearance. Never.

People can choose to have an ugly temper, tell an ugly lie, or be an ugly bully.

Or, people can choose to be tolerant, compassionate, and patient with one another as well as with themselves.

CHAPTER 7

———◦✦◦———

The Heart of Being Vulnerable

Allow yourself to open up your heart to
true intimacy. Be vulnerable to love.

THE VULNERABLE HEART OPENS TO a level of trust that the love of your life will honor your confidences, hopes, and dreams. Once you've been gifted this ultimate degree of intimacy, never, ever mock or use it to hurt. If you should ever betray this trust, don't be naïve when your partner starts shutting down to protect herself or himself from future ridicule.

Once love sparks in your heart, there's always a risk of being hurt. You can *hope* that your lives will always be intimate and comfortable. You can *hope* that your bond is unbreakable. You can *hope* that you will live happily ever after. The truth is that you just don't know. Opening your heart to love armed with only the promise of hope is one of the greatest acts of courage you possibly will ever do.

To be vulnerable is more than sharing daily confidences without knowing they will be honored. Being vulnerable involves finding the deeper truth of your love. Imagine you're lying in bed, each of you wondering if the other would agree to be intimate. Rather than make the first move, do you turn to your side, preferring aloneness rather than the fear of rejection?

Can you be brave enough to know that "Not tonight, honey" doesn't necessarily mean you shouldn't hug, cuddle, snuggle, rub a tired back, or apply lotion to weary feet? Are you comfortable enough with each other to accept that sometimes a gentle touch is enough? To freely allow your loved one to know the intimate you is to know that your feelings, thoughts, and weaknesses are fully accepted with total honesty and that you do not fear judgment because of them.

To be vulnerable in love is one of the most precious gifts you could possibly share with another human being. When your heart is open and vulnerable with your love, you're truly and fully able to realize love's richest rewards.

PART 2
Being Mindful

The art of being mindful is being fully present regardless of where you are or what you're doing. When you're eating, eat. When you're listening, listen. When you're praying, pray. When you're making love, make love.

While I was driving in winter darkness to join a group meditation, my GPS led me on a merry-go-round trip that took twice as long as it should have, with multiple turns on unmarked snow covered country roads. I felt as if I was in the Twilight Zone. By the time I arrived, my nerves were shattered! I couldn't wait to settle in and transcend.

But instead of meditating, all I could think about was my miserable road trip and what other route I could take home to avoid the aggravation. Instead of meditating, I was thinking about the future. Me, of all people! I teach mindfulness, and yet there I was, not being mindful at all.

Luckily, mindfulness did kick in. I knew that I needed to change my vibration channel. As soon as I switched from anxiety to being fully present, I was able to release my navigational frustration and fall into the grace of gratitude. Breathe in. Breathe out. After the jumbled thoughts had been released through meditation, I was able to think clearly and calmly, and then I was able to find the best route home.

For mindfulness to occur, you must have the desire and willingness to change your vibration channel. It's as easy as making a conscious choice to change the channel on your remote. So, in order to manifest change in your life, you need to know that understanding has to start with the level of perception. Change the vibration channel; change your life.

What does being mindful of your partner look like to you? Are you empathetic of her mood? Have you noticed if he looks tired? Did you notice her new haircut? Is he wearing mismatched socks? Does she have lipstick on her teeth? Is there toilet paper on his shoe, or a button missing from her coat?

When you're with your partner, *be* with your partner. *Be* attentive. *Be* fully present. *Be* mindful.

CHAPTER 8

—————⋅❧⋅❦⋅—————

Appreciation Raises Happiness Levels

Tell your partner something that
he or she did for you and why you appreciate it.

TODAY'S WORLD IS HECTIC. WITH everything going on in the world, how can you possibly be expected to make time to show appreciation when you barely have time to whiten your teeth?

At first, appreciation time may seem a little silly after you've already said thank you once. But appreciation takes gratitude one step further by adding *why* an action or expression was so meaningful to you. For example, "I really appreciated that extra cup of coffee. You had perfect timing and brought it just as I needed a pick-me-up."

Each time you show appreciation, positive neural pathways light up in your partner's brain like a fireworks display. These pathways become embedded memories in the subconscious mind. Once these pathways are established, every time you offer appreciation and gratitude, more positive patterns are created. It's like having a time-release capsule that causes one word of appreciation to be like yelling "Bingo!" causing a complete chain reaction of grateful chemicals to brighten the brain with happiness.

These feel-good chemicals are conveniently located in the brain of every human being. Their names are dopamine, oxytocin, serotonin, and endorphins (a group of peptides). An easy way to remember them is by using the anagram DOSE. These particular chemicals are found in the neurotransmitters of the brain that work with receptors to produce positive thoughts, feelings, and actions. Although they are all considered to be "happy chemicals," dopamine is the one member of the feel-good chemicals that is usually given credit for that rush of high you feel after holding the door for the old lady or donating to your favorite charity.

In other words, dopamine is an innate feel-good messenger of the brain that keeps increasing every time you perform *any* act of kindness, even a smile. It can't help itself! As the dopamine level increases, so does your level of happiness and self-confidence.

To amplify that dopamine feeling, start by eating certain foods—bananas, almonds, and dark chocolate. Another way is to have an orgasm. But since it isn't likely—or practical—to go through your day eating bananas and having orgasms, a much simpler way of boosting your happy chemicals is to show appreciation.

Yep, through appreciation time, whenever you offer praise and say *why* you feel grateful, your dopamine level receives an upbeat message, improving the chances of increased kindnesses in order for the brain's neurotransmitters to release more natural chemical bliss. All you have to do is say something nice.

Stacey and Mike agree: "Our marriage is about love, respect, gratitude, and having fun. We have daily and weekly rituals, such as a long hug and kisses every morning with well wishes for the day. And we share a reason why we love each other every Sunday night before bed without repeating a previous reason."

By being appreciative for all the goodness and love in your life, you never know where it may lead. Adopt this motto: Be kind—get a zing of dopamine!

CHAPTER 9

———— ·❖· ————

The Season of Expectations

Create and share a practical, reasonable,
and absurd list of expectations.
Discuss and compromise.
When the time comes, keep your word.

HAVING EXPECTATIONS ABOUT OTHER PEOPLE is like parking your new car at the far edge of the parking lot—there are no guarantees against dents, but you've done what you can to prevent them. Rather than assume expectations of your spouse, keep in mind that to "assume" means to make an "ass" out of "u" and "me."

Some couples automatically have many expectations—honesty, sharing the workload, fiscal responsibility, emotional support, shared aspirations, and a lifetime of warm and caring affection. But when it comes to day-to-day living—entertainment; activities; attending events like weddings, birthdays, sports, concerts; spending time with family members and friends—some expectations may be considered to be in the gray area.

Many of these expectations can be hashed out ahead of time by making a list of what-if questions. Have an open discussion about situations, mixing the absurd with what's likely possible. Assume nothing, and you can actually have fun with it.

Before you get started, each of you should create a personal basic list of scenarios based on the what-if questions you came up with together. Then, exchange your lists and write your responses—no sneak peeks. Now compare your answers and decide what is and isn't negotiable. Cross your fingers and hope that your expectations match.

Just in case you're stuck, here are a few what-ifs to get you started:

What if ...

- A stray dog or cat comes into your life. Do you keep it? Find it a home? Leave it alone? Take it to a shelter?

- The Super Bowl or the last game of the Stanley Cup finals is the same day as a best friend's birthday party? Do you go to the party or stay home and watch the game? Does it make a difference if your home town team is playing?

- Your wife's friend needs to move, and she's offered your help without asking. Do you help her friend move? Are there any exceptions?

- Your colleagues invite you to happy hour after work. You told your partner that you'd come directly home, but you've had a rough day and welcome the chance to unwind. What do you do?

- Your in-laws are flying in from out of town and want to stay with you. Your space is large enough for them to stay. Is that okay with you? What if space is limited?

- Your partner's favorite musical group comes to town. You don't really much care for them. Do you attend or tell her to find someone else to go with?

- You have a difficult day at work and come home to a sink full of dishes and a messy house even though your partner has been home all day doing nothing. Do you say anything?

- You're passionate about saving the animals and the environment and addressing the issue of global warming. Your partner isn't. Are you okay with that?

- Your partner makes a frivolous purchase that the family budget can't afford. Can you deal with that?

- You exercise and eat well, but your partner doesn't take self-care seriously. Can you handle that?

- There's a family function—wedding or birthday. Do you go even if you don't want to?

- Your partner wants to spend every weekend with his or her family. Is that okay with you?

- An old boyfriend or girlfriend comes into town and wants to meet for lunch. Do you accept the invitation?

- There's a neighborhood picnic. Do you both want to participate?

Those are just examples of a few of the more common what-ifs that couples must deal with. I'm certain that you can add a lot more that fit your lifestyle or expectations.

Compromise is always expected when you're married, whether it's taking turns doing chores or deciding which movie to watch. Just be careful that it doesn't reach the point of being too one sided. Because, when the solution is no longer a compromise, it crosses over into the land of resentment. You can always revisit your list of expectations from time to time as situations arise and make adjustments.

Camille was still working when her husband retired. Since retiring, he's volunteered to do the grocery shopping and cook dinner. When I asked if he was a good cook, she laughed. "Well, after years of having to rush home to start dinner, I don't care if we have hot dogs every night. I have no expectations—there's no complaining here. I never expected that he would take over the cooking like he did!"

When my favorite duo, Simon and Garfunkel, came to Pittsburgh for a concert, I assumed that my husband would go with me. After he flatly refused, I asked friends, but no one could make it. At the time, I didn't have the confidence to drive downtown by myself, so I foolishly missed my one opportunity to see them perform and experience the electrifying energy only felt at concerts.

A couple of months later, Rodney Dangerfield came to Pittsburgh, and my husband wanted to see him. Naturally, I acted in a mature manner, and, of course, I said no! I thought that by refusing to go, I was teaching him a lesson. I imagined that he would feel the same disappointment that I felt when he wouldn't go to the Simon and Garfunkel concert with me. Turns out, he didn't care. Instead, he went golfing. Whatever could I have been thinking? For some reason, things often sound better in theory than actual practice.

When I asked Norine to offer sage wisdom after decades of being married to Greg, she quickly answered, "Patience. Greg is extremely patient. He even said that he would have divorced me long ago but he saw how hard I worked at improving myself. I mean, I know how difficult I was! Thank goodness for Greg's patience." She continued, "No, wait a minute … it's acceptance. That's it. Greg accepts me for who I am. He is such a good man. This morning, for example, he knew that I wanted to come to this talk about mindfulness, so he offered to drive my mother to church. I told him she could miss *one* Sunday, but instead of trying to make me feel guilty, he accepted that I wanted to come to the meeting and offered to take her. That's just who he is. No, let me change that again … it's expectations. He has no expectations of me, and I don't have any of him. When we first moved to Pittsburgh, we released all expectations of what life would be like here. I'm a fanatical Pirate fan, and Greg's always reminding me to just enjoy the game—don't have expectations of how they do; just enjoy watching them. It's the same with us. We live in the now without expectations of each other, just doing the best we can to make life easier. I just feel really lucky to have found Greg." Norine nodded. "Yes, I'm grateful. I guess we're both lucky." She smiled as though confirming it in her mind that she's covered all the bases.

Just as seasons change, so do the circumstances of your marriage. As years pass, you mature together and expectations change. So revisit and update your expectation list as needed. If everything is running smoothly and you decide it's no longer needed, simply throw it away.

There is one thing that you can always expect in life if you pay attention:

You can always expect miracles.

CHAPTER 10

---◆◇◆---

The Grace of Giving and Receiving

The more you give from your heart,
the more your heart receives in grace.

AS THE SUN AND RAIN give life to the trees and plants, the trees and plants receive with grace and, in return, provide food, shelter, and shade. To live in the grace of giving and receiving, couples need only to observe nature to find the balance of love.

When there's a sense of equal balance, there's a natural exchange of love, not obligation. Couples who contribute to the stability of their relationship by sharing in the entire workload have an attitude that speaks to each partner's personal give-and-receive philosophy: "I listen and speak to you with respect, and you listen and speak to me with respect." What could be simpler?

Be wary of anyone who keeps score of who did what and when. The agenda of someone who says "I did this for you, now it's your turn to do something for me" is a person who keeps upping the ante. This attitude encourages the backdoor belief expressed in the saying "I'll scratch your back, but first, you have to scratch mine." The act of keeping score is a seesaw of guilt that causes the receiver to feel that he or she is always in payback mode.

Whenever one partner plays the role of the rational adult and the other behaves with antics of a spoiled child, it's impossible to have a natural balance. Be mindful that, if one of you is constantly giving, sacrificing, and forgiving more than the other, a cauldron of smoldering anger and resentment is brewing more fumes than are produced by moonshine whiskey.

The next time a little kid with a toothy smile holds the door open for you at the store, notice how you feel by this spontaneous show of consideration. He doesn't ask for anything in return but a simple "thank you." Watch the grin of self-satisfaction that is the result of simply knowing that a simple act of kindness has helped someone. As this child grows, he'll open many doors, hold many umbrellas, and receive much gratitude. He has already learned the grace of giving and receiving. Someday, there will be a little kid to hold open the door for him.

Jamie says, "Adam and I balance each other out. For example, when I'm feeling down or discouraged, Adam always finds a way to make me laugh, and I do the same for him. Our basic philosophy is "what's mine is his and what's yours is mine." We don't pay attention to the small stuff. We give and take equally." Adam adds, "We know that we can count on each other, no matter what."

Once you make the commitment to be thoughtful and considerate, the noise and silence you experience in your journey together won't matter. You'll stay on the path of giving and receiving by creating a lifetime of balance and love.

CHAPTER 11

———— ⟡ ————

Living in Gratitude

*Having gratitude in your heart
raises your spiritual vibration and
invites abundance into your life.
Gratitude is a magical word.*

COMPLAINT IS LIKE WATER; IT follows the path of least resistance. To live in gratitude takes mindful thought. Once the tiniest glimpse of gratefulness is offered in place of complaint, "happy chemicals" are activated in the brain, there's a vibrational shift to a higher level, and there's an awareness of all the wonderfulness in your life, however small.

What's the difference between gratitude and gratefulness? Gratitude is to awaken each day with thankfulness in your heart. It's like saying, "Thank you, Divine Creator, for another day." Gratefulness is how you live your life. It's to live without complaint and not take everyday blessings for granted.

When you're in the midst of chaos, dark energy can easily take control of your subconscious mind. In order to recover the lightness of gratitude, call upon your inner strength for guidance. Once the lens of perception changes from sadness to gratefulness, the mind opens up, inspiration takes hold, and the quality of your life improves. Some people feel an immediate shift of positive energy, while for others, the change may take longer based on a tribal belief system and level of willingness to surrender.

If finding gratitude is a struggle, start with the basics: "I'm grateful to see the smile of my love and feel the touch of his arms." "I'm grateful for the unconditional love she gives to me."

Think of gratitude as an energy drink, creating emotions that automatically ignite positive energies. These energies then release the feel-good chemical dopamine to your brain. Dopamine is increased through diet, pleasurable activities, kindnesses, and replacing that need to complain with thankfulness. Regardless of what pressures or problems are happening in your life, by forcing yourself to speak from a place of gratitude, you will be bound to arouse positive feelings.

Here are some suggestions to help you live in gratitude:

- Join a gratitude meetup group in your area. Meetup groups can be found on the internet. Like-minded people can help keep you on track.

- Keep a gratitude journal. Even if you can't find a meetup group near you, keep a gratitude journal for your own satisfaction. You can find ready-made journals, or you can make your own, even using a simple notebook. All you need to do is to write, once or twice a week, something as simple as "I'm grateful for the gift of Simon and Garfunkel music." "I'm grateful for clean water." "I'm grateful the store has toilet paper." "I'm grateful for our healthcare workers." Gratefulness can be as mundane or as profound as you want it to be.

- Mark on your calendar your gratitude level today from one to ten. Throughout the day, consciously offer gratitude in place of complaint. Practice, practice, practice until gratitude becomes a habit. As soon as a thought of complaint or judgment enters, replace it with gratitude, no matter how minor you think that it is.

- Practice being grateful in place of being aggravated. For example, if you're stuck in construction traffic (which in Pittsburgh happens year round, so I get plenty of practice), gratitude says, "I'm grateful I have enough gas. I'm grateful there isn't an accident. I'm grateful to have someplace to go. I am grateful the roads are being repaired. I'm grateful that there are jobs being provided to the workmen."

- Keep a daily tally sheet with two columns. In one column, list the number of times you complained, passed judgment, or made a negative comment. In the second column, keep track of the number of times you expressed thankfulness, offered a kind word, or lent a helping hand. Once gratitude is integrated into your life, you become aware of the grace that surrounds you.

Writing about gratefulness cements the words into positive emotions. To live a life of gratitude makes us aware that we must not to dwell in self-pity. When I was a teenager, I was a complaining one day about how I didn't like the bump on my nose. My dad wrote this on a piece of paper and handed it to me: "I once complained I had no shoes until I met a man who had no feet." I stopped complaining.

Caryl emphasizes the positive side of life: "We don't let the little things bother us. We're grateful for the love we share, and we don't take each other for granted. We honestly connect with humor and enjoy being spontaneous."

The time to be grateful is *now*. Once you become mindful of how much energy we waste when we spend time in complaint and negativity, making the change to devote more time into creating a better and more desirable future is as effortless as breathing.

Today, right now, hold gratitude in your heart. Take your loved one's face in your hands, look deeply into his or her, eyes and say, "I'm grateful to have you in my life."

May you always live in God's grace and hold gratitude within your heart.

Cultivate the habit of being grateful for every good thing that comes to you, and to give thanks continuously. And because all things have contributed to your advancement, you should include all things in your gratitude.

Ralph Waldo Emerson

CHAPTER 12

—⟨⊰•⊱⟩—

The Honor Code

Honor your partner by choosing a
noble code of conduct to live by 24/7.
Honor your partner through thoughts, words, and deeds.
Be mindful to never take each other for granted.

"LOVE, HONOR, AND CHERISH" ARE more than just ordinary words somberly spoken during a sacred wedding ceremony. These are words that confirm a lifelong commitment to have and to hold love in your life.

Close your eyes. Take a deep breath and slowly repeat each word. Speak to your heart: "Love. Honor. Cherish." Sense how these three innocent words offer vibrational power and a sense of being uplifted.

To *love* is to accept someone unconditionally, despite known flaws.

To *honor* is to have and to hold the upmost respect for each other moment by moment, day in and day out, year after year. Some people think that to honor means to place your love on a pedestal, but that isn't realistic, is it? After all, pedestals have a tendency to topple, while honor stands tall and strong.

To *cherish* is to promise caring and gentle nurture during the twists and turns along the pathways of life, paying no heed to how narrow the alley or how wide the gulf.

To honor your relationship is to act accordingly—love, honor, cherish—whether at home, at work, or out with friends, both in private and public. It's an ethical code of conduct of principled actions that knows no boundaries. If you're with a group of friends and they're spewing complaints about their spouses or significant others, do you join in or speak about your life partner with tenderness, love, and appreciation?

"How would I feel if my husband talked the same way about me?" "If she heard me, would she be embarrassed and hurt or would she feel loved and honored?" "How will I feel if I betray his confidence?" "What would he think of me if he knew that I betrayed his confidence?" When speaking and acting with a sense of honor, you're holding yourself, your partner, and your relationship in the highest esteem.

A person who embraces honor has patience. When you speak well of your partner, with genuine and sincere feelings, she'll know it and feel it, even if she isn't present to hear your words. If you speak mockingly of him, with disrespect and sarcastic tone, hurt feelings are sure to sneak into every aspect of your marriage.

Of course, if there's a humorous story that you just have to tell, make certain that your partner is laughing, too, and it's not told to cause embarrassment. Jim would affectionately call my sister, Colette, "Lucy," referring to the *I Love Lucy* character, whenever she did or said something silly. Colette had a great sense of humor and would laugh along with him, as she did when Jim was working in a country in Europe. They were talking on the phone when Colette asked him where he would be eating Thanksgiving dinner. He said, "Oh, Lucy, I don't think they have Thanksgiving here!" I can still hear her contagious laugh as she repeated the story.

Treat your partner as though he or she is the most precious gift in your life. When he's thought of as though he's more valuable than a Rembrandt painting, or she feels as prized as a Babe Ruth autographed baseball, you honor each other.

Honor is what makes love priceless!

CHAPTER 13

————⚬⟨❊⟩⚬————

How Can I Help?

"What can I do to help?" This is a powerful question.
Working together reduces stress, makes the time go faster,
makes tasks less tedious, and achieves mutual satisfaction.

CRASH! THE HALLWAY CEILING INTIMATELY met the floor below in one heap of plaster rubble! Like Humpty Dumpty, the ceiling was done for. It could not be put back together. But I had an even bigger problem than a hole in the ceiling. How on earth was I going to afford to have it repaired?

Then I remembered my friend telling me how her handyman husband needed a project, and, as luck would have it, here was one right on my hallway floor. Goodness knows that I'm always happy to oblige!

When they arrived, my friend told me that she liked to help her husband, serving as a second pair of hands. I admired how they worked together while she did a variety of tasks—steadying the ladder, handing him tools, and, after the job was done, using the shop-vac for clean-up while he packed away his tools. Then, when all was done, we were able to have a relaxing visit.

"How can I help?" is a welcomed phrase, whether painting a room, vacuuming, folding clothes, or raking leaves, and there are multiple ways to provide a lending hand.

If your partner's the clueless type who doesn't think to offer help, ask for it. Once you have asked, if you're scoffed at or ignored, look for deeper issues. Is your partner lazy, legitimately tired, unmotivated, or just uncaring? Is the request unreasonable? Could she be an over-the-top perfectionist and nothing you do is ever right? Is he too prideful to accept help? Does he prefer to be the martyr so he can boast about his greatness?

Regardless of being asked or not, if you see that your partner's flushed and rushing around, don't just sit there aimlessly switching channels on the remote. Turn off the TV, shut down the computer, and hang up the phone. Show that you're ready to pitch in! Stop waiting to be asked. Look around and think for yourself: Load the dishwasher, move the clothes from the washer into the dryer, peel the potatoes, set the table, vacuum, fix the beds, take out the garbage. Get off your duff and just do it!

It's the thoughtful little things that count the most. When your partner brings work home from her job, she may request that you do something as small as turning the volume down on the TV, making a snack, or engaging the kids in a quiet activity. Sometimes he just wants to let off some steam about his job and needs an attentive listener to help him see things from a fresh perspective. By being observant and empathetic of your partner's needs, regardless of the task, job, or chore, offering to help in any small way shows that you care.

PART 3

Mindful Communication

Be mindful of nonverbal cues. Here are some examples:

- Does the situation match the body language?
- What is the antecedent of the comment or gesture? Is there an event taking place?
- Where is the location that it occurred? What are the circumstances?
- Are the non-verbal cues sending the same message?
- Is the person leaning away or leaning in?
- Are the hands clenched or open?
- Is there a relaxed smile, a fake smile, a smirk or a frown?
- Are the feet pointing toward you or the exit?
- Are lips pursed? Does the face look like it's thinking, frustrated, or angry?
- Do the tone of voice and body language match with what's being said?
- Do you observe tapping of feet, hands in pockets, palms up, or arms folded?
- Is what is being said in alignment with one's culture?
- Is there bowing, hugging, kissing, fist bumping, elbow touching, or shaking of hands?
- Is this how the person generally behaves when happy, excited, tired, frustrated, hungry, or bored?

CHAPTER 14

·⟨⟩·⟨⟩·

Respectful Communication Rocks!

*The spoken word, tone of voice, and
nonverbal body language cues all add
up to mindful communication.*

A RAISED EYEBROW OR PURSED lips says a lot more than words.
Body movements and positioning, facial expressions, and gestures can
either rock your marriage or be the tipping point to its destruction.
Respectful communication is more important than flushable toilets!

To rock your world, how well do you communicate? When face to
face with your loved one, realize that words are only a fraction of the
message. For example, imagine your loved ones expressions when you
say the words *I love you* using different tones of voice.

"I LOVE YOU"—Shouting it for all the world to know.

"I love you."—Whispered with tenderness, close up and personal.

51

"I love you …"—A slight pause may mean there's a "but" coming afterwards.

"I love **you?**"—Could mean, "What makes you *think* that I love *you?*"

"I love *you?*"—Of course I love you! How could you even ask?

"**I** love you."—I'm the one who truly loves you.

"I love **YOU!**"—And no one else.

Much communication is done subconsciously through involuntary body movements including facial expressions and hand or arm gestures. Can you control a blush? It's the same thing. Body movements are louder than words. One way to tell if a couple is simpatico is to notice how each partner's movements are often mirrored by the other.

You may have heard the wise old advice to think before you speak. This bodes well when being diplomatic with a loved one. How many times have you heard someone say, "That sounded better in my head"? By gathering your thoughts and thinking them all the way through before the words leave your lips, you'll become more aware of involuntary movements or gestures. There's a knack to being honest and tactful while, at the same time getting your message across.

What about communicating via yelling? Practically everyone yells at some point, often out of frustration or to emphasize a point. However, yelling or screaming at someone you love out of habit induces fear and lessens the message. Sometimes yelling can be useful when immediate results are necessary. An example is a coach yelling from the sidelines. But after the game, talking calmly to players one-on-one is what gets results in the long term.

Keep personal matters personal and private matters private. Discussing private stuff in front of others or posting personal arguments on the internet is embarrassing, unnecessary, and makes you look petty and insecure. Besides, it's almost certain to come back and bite you in the butt. Be careful what you want the world to see. What you write may give the wrong impression and lead to embarrassment and hurt feelings.

Choosing the right time for any important discussion makes sense. Would you ask your wife about buying a new tractor during lovemaking? Of course not! That's like trimming your toenails with hedge clippers. Ask yourself, when would be a good time to talk about buying a tractor?

Be aware of your hand gestures, which can create or emphasize your message. For example, when you want to make a point and emphasize your words, stay away from using a pointing finger. Your partner may interpret the pointed index finger as an accusation or criticism, which might trigger a negative response. Instead, use the full hand, like in a karate chop position. Many hands gestures have various meanings in different cultures, so become aware of what your hands are saying— wherever you are.

It doesn't take a private detective to figure out the clues for how you can improve your overall communication skills. Your perception of what's being said and how it's said is valuable when assessing your personal style. This takes patience, practice, and mindfulness!

Respectful communication rocks powerful mojo!

CHAPTER 15

———◈◆◈———

ABCs of Arguing

Attack the topic or problem, not the person.
Be willing to maintain an open mind.
Children need to be totally out of earshot
and never involved.
Do keep focused on the issue at hand.
Examine your role in the argument
and take ownership of your words.
Frequently and fully, remember to breathe.
Give your partner time to respond.

DISAGREEMENTS ARE AS NATURAL TO couples as apples are to pie. As for me, arguing has never been one of my strong points. I'm just not one of those people with the witty comeback or a touché moment. For days, I struggle to think of the perfect comment, and by then, it falls to the wayside like a lump of coal. What a waste of valuable time and brain energy.

There are couples who argue all the time, couples who argue some of the time, and couples who don't argue at all. But most couples agree that arguing is an important part of clearing the air, justifying opinions, stating frustrations, and being able to verbally relay needs and desires. That is, of course, as long as there is respect.

Bonnie and her husband have very few disagreements. Nevertheless, they decided to take a professional approach to learn how to fight fair. "Jim and I rarely argue, but when we do, my warrior-self comes out in full force, and Jim retreats to the hills," Bonnie said. "While I demand immediate resolution, Jim requires time to consider all options before responding. While I was making demands of Jim when I was in my 'warrior' mode, Jim, feeling under attack, wasn't able to think clearly." Through counseling, Jim learned to tell Bonnie that he needed more time to think.

Bonnie learned to ask, "How much time do you need?" Once he said, "Four days." "I said 'No way! I need resolution before that!' So we compromised that he would have a response in two days. Two days is okay. I can keep my emotions in check for two days, but not four!"

Bonnie explained how the counselor guided them to examine their fighting techniques. While Bonnie continues to be the warrior, she now knows that Jim needs time to fully consider his response. By the time his processing limit is due, Bonnie is calmer and ready to listen to what he has to say. Jim is then able to present his side of the argument in a rational way. Resolutions are made and peace is restored.

I spoke with Bonnie a few months after she shared her story and asked her how she was doing with her inner warrior. She smiled. "Great! And now it's even better since I learned to meditate every day."

Disagreements are healthy ways to bring problems into the open rather than harboring resentment. It's also stimulating to be able to have an honest and forthright discussion about opinions and ideas. But when a disagreement turns ugly and anger escalates to the point that you say mean things you can't erase, it's time to take notice.

Try putting yourself in your partner's shoes by closing your eyes and imagining the weight of angry words pounding on your skin. See the words thoughtlessly hanging in the heaviness of the atmosphere, leaving a psychic path of physical havoc in its wake. 'It felt like I was *hit* in the gut." "It was like a *slap* to my face." "I've been *stabbed* in the back."

Each time you have an argument that turns into rage, the brain acts like an elevator, pushing buttons to a higher floor every time you enter, escalating the level of anger. By the time you reach the top floor, the brain's been trained to have a "short fuse." This level of anger becomes an "anger rut" in your brain. To rewire this rut, you must take conscious control by using empowering language like "I am in control of myself" or "I choose to be patient."

Before reaching the place of no return, force yourself to stop. Take a deep breath. Be mindful of your words and emotions. Realize that, right or wrong, mistakes are made, opinions are formed, and your perceptions are your own making.

Taking control with your conscious thoughts isn't as hard as you may think. It's as simple as changing the frequency on your radio, where *you* have the power to determine your tune, volume, and channel.

In order to gain control of your inborn sense of fair play, follow the basic ABCs of arguing:

Attack the topic, not the person. If your partner makes family comparisons, screaming things like "You're just like your father (or mother)!" what is he or she really saying? What about it makes you so uncomfortable? Is he or she pushing your buttons to get a reaction?

Be willing to maintain an open mind and listen to the other person's perspective. Release the need to win at any cost. Accept that you're not always right.

Children need to be totally *out* of earshot. Kids have super-sonic hearing and can hear every argument through the floor registers. Heat and air registers are gateways that carry sound throughout the house. Never, ever involve the kids. It's not their fault, so do not bring them into it.

Do keep focused on the issue at hand. Acknowledge that individuals can have differences of opinions and are still valued.

Examine your role in the argument and take ownership of your words. By preserving respect for each other, no one will be walking on hot coals the next time something happens. Be respectful of feelings and not a proponent of name-calling.

Frequently and fully, remember to breathe.

Give time to respond. Some people need time to think about an appropriate response.

Have the willpower to keep your arguments private. You'll make up and forget, while others, especially family members, remember.

I am in control: "It's not personal" must become your slogan.

Justify your position without playing the righteousness card.

Key to resolution is to find a solution.

Leave it to a counselor if professional guidance is needed. He or she may offer a fresh perspective.

Maintain a neutral perspective. Be aware not everyone has your point of view.

Never attack your partner's character. This can be considered as emotional abuse.

Offer to take a step back to cool down. Let your partner know when you need to retreat and that you'll be back when you're calmer. This is not to be confused with the sulking or the silent treatment.

Personal attacks are toxic to the relationship.

Questions should never be asked that you don't want to hear the answer to. For example, "Have you gambled our rent money?" Even if he lies, you'll know the truth. If the rent money has been lost, what do you intend to do about it? What consequences are you prepared to enforce?

Remember that you love each other. This love will help you to reach a resolution. Arguing simply is a means to help your relationship grow.

Stay in present time to seek a solution. "Do what you've always done, and get what you've always got." This saying rings true when you keep rehashing the same conflict.

Table discussions for another day when they get too overheated. Sometimes it takes time to process what's been said, and it's okay to reschedule.

Ultimatums are never spoken unless you plan to act on them. Think carefully before you say something you'll regret.

Visualize the weight of your words. Value what your partner has to say.

Winning the argument isn't the goal. Don't make it about ego.

X—being an ex isn't all that it's cracked up to be, so learn how to cooperate.

Y are you really arguing? What are the true underlying issues?

Zen approach to conflict includes patience, understanding, and compassion.

As you take self-inventory of your personal arguing techniques, consider yourself as having the skill of negotiating a compromise and release your sense of being prideful. No one wants to be thought of as unfair. When you take control of your anger, your relationship is the true winner.

CHAPTER 16

---⬥❧❧❦⬥---

Skills to Fight Right

Speak using "I" statements. Seek resolution.
Accept that you're not always right.
This is not a competition. This is marriage.

LET'S TAKE ARGUMENTS A STEP further: There are distinct ways to fight right. While it isn't the disagreement that's concerning, it's the escalation of anger to the point of no return that couples need to watch out for. Once your awareness is raised by knowing, understanding, and honoring how to fight right, pettiness and hurt feelings are preventable and disagreements can be resolved.

Most of the guidelines are common sense, and a few may be a little repetitive but still serve as reminders to speak to the importance of maintaining dignity. They are listed here in no particular order.

Here are the most common fight right dos and don'ts:

- Do stay in the present. Focus on what your partner is saying.

- Do be watchful of body language.

- Do ask yourself, "Why am I really angry?" Look for underlying causes.

- Do focus on one issue at a time. If something else arises, make an appointment to tackle that one another day, another time. Remain on course to resolve the current issue.

- Do set boundaries ahead of time as to what information you're willing to share with others. Recognize when the argument has run its course and has come to an end. There's no gain in continuing an argument once a conclusion has been reached.

- Do take responsibility for your role in the disagreement to demonstrate honesty and trust. This is *not* the same as accepting misplaced blame for something you didn't do.

- Do stick to the subject at hand. You're seeking a peaceful resolution, not instigating a war dance. Stay on topic. Don't let your ego get the best of you.

- Do take a break and rest. Set a timer if you have to. Twenty minutes is a good length of time for preventing escalation. Revisit the issue at a later time either on the same day or on another as long as you have time to think about the conflict and ways to resolve it.

- Do take advantage of the cooling-down time by taking deep breaths. Make certain to let your partner know that you're removing yourself to calm down, not as a silent treatment. Meditation and quiet reflection also help in the process.

- Do know what you want to accomplish.

- Do accept an apology with grace if it is sincerely offered. Allow your partner to maintain dignity. Note that this does not include the pattern of physical abuse where you need to remove yourself.

- Do remember what's important for the marriage. It's not a competition, and it's not about ego.

- Do go to bed angry rather than rehashing until dawn. Everything looks better in the morning, and you'll look at the issue with a fresh perspective. Staying up all night results in a foggy brain when a clear head is needed to reach an amiable resolution. Keep pen and pencil on the nightstand to write down any pertinent thoughts that come to you during the night.

- Do keep your arguments private. While you're most likely to kiss and make up, your friends and family will remember every incident and form negative opinions. Unless there's a threat of harm to self or others, keep it to yourselves.

- Do take responsibility for your actions.

- Do keep your promises. Your word is your bond. Keep honor by being honest.

- Do speak the truth, even if it hurts or isn't what your partner wants to hear. Lies have a tendency to come back and bite you in the butt.

- Do speak respectfully. This is a person you love. Disrespect says more about you.

- Do use your "I" statements because they offer insight into the "real" you, especially your vulnerabilities. Be specific. For example: "I feel unappreciated when I cook a nice dinner and you don't call that you're working late."

- Do ask questions and clarify anything you don't understand.

- Don't ever fight in front of the kids! Period. You can imagine (or maybe remember) how scared a kid feels when parents are screaming and calling each other names. A careless and selfish three-second comment could cause permanent emotional damage. Floor registers are like telegraphs through which words travel quickly.

- Don't involve family. Know what is and isn't appropriate to be shared. Later, you'll kiss and make up, but they *will* remember.

- Don't involve friends or ask them to take sides. Telling your friends about every little thing usually makes matters worse. Friends are often quick to offer opinions, but that doesn't mean they are the right ones.

- Don't air your disagreements on social media. No one wants to read about your family secrets.

- Don't fight in public. It's embarrassing and uncomfortable for everyone.

- Don't hit below the belt by bringing up something told in confidence.

- Don't bring up the past. What's the point? It's done. Let it go.

- Don't use sarcasm. It shows lack of respect and can be hurtful.

- Don't push buttons or instigate. Instead, choose to change your attitude.

- Don't presume to be a mind reader and know what your partner is thinking.

- Don't resort to "bully" behavior like name-calling, character bashing, or making threats.

- Don't use put-downs, obscenities, or degrading comments. Never use the "D" word to gain leverage or for shock value. Once it's out there, it's hard to take back.

I don't know anyone who enjoys being criticized, even if they ask for an honest opinion. Yet criticism is often the root cause of arguments. So if you ever have the need to criticize, stop and decide if your words are useful and tactful.

Here are the three Cs to consider when giving feedback:

> Constructive: Choose the timing. Imagine how embarrassing it would be to tell a spouse at a dinner party, "For crying out loud! Stop slurping your soup! You're such a pig!" Some things are best to be said in private or not at all.

> Compassionate: Phrase the criticism in a statement that will not arouse a defensive reaction by using your "I" statements: "I feel embarrassed when you slurp your soup because its poor manners, and I know that you take pride in being appropriate." Be assertive but kind.

> Consistent: Avoid confusion. It's either acceptable or not. In other words, don't laugh at soup slurping one day and find it inappropriate the next.

Setting boundaries can be a challenge, but once you learn to communicate like a mature adult, you'll feel better about yourself and your relationship. Resolution will be faster, positive feelings will remain intact, and your marriage will be the true winner.

CHAPTER 17

——— ❧•❧ ———

Listen to Hear

Practice being a reflective listener.
Clarify what you hear by asking questions.
Show empathy to the intensity of emotions.
Watch for nonverbal clues.
A loved one needs to trust to truly being heard.

WHAT WORD HAS TWO EYES and says "I care?" Listening. It seems obvious, but listening to your partner with your full attention really does send the "I care" message loud and clear.

Whether listening to the melody of a songbird, the rhythm of the ocean's waves, or the lyrics of a love song, listening is a fundamental skill to navigate through the sounds of caring.

When listening to a loved one, let him or her know that you are hearing every word. Mindful listening requires patience and practice. You must be patient to know when to speak, when to be quiet, and in today's world, when it's appropriate to text or send an email. To truly listen, you must suspend your own opinions and judgments and let your partner know that you understand what he or she has to say. This is best done during face-to-face discussions. Accurate listening often requires *seeing* the facial expressions and *hearing* the tone of voice.

To be a reflective listener, make a conscious effort to remove any distractions: clear your mind, uncross your arms, make eye contact, and, for goodness sake, silence your cell phone. This is not the time to be checking text messages or going through email. Simply pay attention to body language, posture, and tone of voice. Be empathetic. Listen for the true message and ask clarifying questions.

Being mindful also acknowledges that not everyone is skilled at being an effective listener. For example, notice of the length of the listener's attention span. If you're the one speaking, be watchful for glazed-over eyes. You know the look—the one that indicates that the mind's ability to concentrate has elapsed. The blank face doesn't mean that you're intentionally being ignored; it's just that the person simply and legitimately cannot focus any longer. What's the length of time that you're able to focus before your eyes glaze over?

Learn to be a mindful listener:

- Remove all distractions.

- Look at the speaker. Maintain eye contact.

- Be fully attentive to what's being said.

- Ask clarifying questions so you fully comprehend.

- Don't allow yourself to be attached to your personal opinions. (This one may be the most difficult.)

- Remain open-minded and nonjudgmental.

- Listen with an open heart.

- Notice the emotional mood, posture, body language, tone of voice, and any other non-verbal clues.

When it is your time to speak, repeat what the speaker has said. This is a way to keep you connected and let your partner know that you've been paying attention. If you are confused or you don't understand the meaning of any of the words, ask for further explanation, "I think I understand, but I'm not quite sure of the meaning of _____."

Repeating words in question form is another way to show that you've been listening: Respond to "I have to wake up really early tomorrow" by asking "How early do you have to wake up?" Repeating the words your partner has used builds trust to being heard.

If you truly take the time to listen to the everyday nothingness, then, when the big stuff happens, your partner will trust that he or she will honestly be heard. So when you listen, know that it takes more than your ears to hear what's being said.

Active Listening

Ask questions to clarify and improve understanding.

Don't interrupt, give suggestions, or offer advice.

Just listen!

Be impartial

Don't take sides.

Show nonverbal understanding through gestures and body language.

THANK YOU FOR LISTENING

Put yourself in the other person's place to better understand facts and feelings.

Maintain eye contact.

Do *not* stare or glare!

Restate the most important facts and feelings.

Face the speaker with intent to hear what is being said.

Do *not* talk about *your* feelings or *your* problems.

CHAPTER 18

———— ⟨⟨⟩⟩ ————

The Sounds of Silence

*There are times when it's best
to let your eyes do the listening.
Breathe. Observe the tone of voice,
choice of words, and body language.*

"YOU CAN'T PUT YOUR FOOT in your mouth if your mouth closed!" This is sound advice for anyone. When you don't say anything at all, you can't be misquoted, can't be embarrassed, and can't be rude.

Although there are many different types of scenarios, let's explore one in which your partner comes to you with a problem at work. The first thing for you to do is to figure out what role you're expected to play:

- Do you need to just listen and be a sounding board to test the validity of ideas?

- Do you need to play devil's advocate to help strengthen a debate?

- Do you need to support ownership of a decision about finding a solution?

- Are you outwardly being asked to offer your opinion and/ or advice?

By being mindfully silent, you'll be able to sense what course is needed for a successful resolution. Whatever happens, it's important for your partner to know that he or she has been heard and that you've listened with sincere interest.

Knowing when to stay silent means you've conquered the art of self-control. Being silent is a form of hearing that enables you to grasp the nitty-gritty of what's really being said. You can gain valuable insight by maintaining eye contact along with a sense of calm. (This does not include glaring!) When your eyes do the listening, you'll be able to observe body language, gauge emotions and detect slight facial expressions.

The act of being silent is a challenge for most humans. Think about how often you've gotten caught up in your own egoic mind chattering thoughts, ready to jump in at the slightest pause. Are you ready to learn the value of breathing, observing, and thinking before speaking?

One spouse who has been married for over fifty years shared a formula she uses to conquer the skill of listening through silence: "I think a lot of our success is because I filter my thoughts. While I may say something in my head over and over, it never leaves my lips out loud. That way, I feel as though I've released the anger, but now our argument won't escalate into something bigger. By filtering my thoughts, I've been able to stay on topic. Then, what I really say out loud is, 'Do you really think that's a good idea?' Ultimately the situation works its way through to a satisfactory conclusion simply because I've kept my thoughts in check."

Paulette Glover

If interrupting is your usual mode of operation, your partner may not understand the new, improved, listening you. He may feel uncomfortable and wonder what you're up to. He may even ask, "What are you doing?" To which you calmly reply, "I'm listening to you, honey."

Incidentally, if someone is on a rant, telling that person to "calm down" doesn't accomplish anything! With those two words, you are denying the other person's feelings, misunderstanding the other person's emotions, and being condescending. You may be under the perception that you're acting in good faith, but the suggestion to "calm down" may actually escalate the other person's anxiety. Have you ever tried telling the wind to quit blowing?

Instead, take a step back and observe. When it's time, respond with empathy and compassion. "I'm here for you." "I understand." "You're not alone." "I hear you." These are just a few suggestions. Most humans needs to vent at one time or another. Remember that listening with silence is a finely tuned craft.

Just as messages appear in the silence of dreams, they also appear through the silence of observation. Just observe, and you'll be able to clearly hear what's being said. As my dad would say, "Silence doesn't mean that you don't know. Silence means that you are thinking."

CHAPTER 19

—⟨⟩⟨⟩—

Embracing a Safe Environment

*A safe environment is a home without
criticism, rejection, or ridicule.
It builds a foundation of trust that will
grow into love and admiration.*

TO EMBRACE A SAFE HOME environment is to recognize the importance of creating a home where thoughts and dreams are freely discussed regardless of how wild or farfetched they sound. It's a place to talk about your everyday experiences knowing that there won't be any criticism, rejection, interruption, ridicule, or judgment. In other words, a safe environment is a space where kindness and acceptance is maintained at all times.

In a safe environment, you are willing to hear honest opinions and keep confidences as long as there's no threat of physical or emotional harm.[2] If you should ever violate this trust, understand that it may take years to earn it back, if ever you can. Once a confidence is betrayed or something is said that makes your partner look foolish, how can you expect him or her to maintain trust in the future?

Be aware of the spoken words in your home. A safe environment recognizes the need to stay emotionally nourished. Every person must fully understand the boundaries of tolerance. It's a place where all members know that positive healthy joking is uplifting, and negative mean teasing isn't tolerated.

By creating a safe environment from the onset, each family member is confident, knowing that

no matter what he or she has to say, love and acceptance has the highest priority.

---

[2] The only time it is acceptable to expose a confidence is if it contains information that could result in harming of self or another. At that time, professional help should be sought immediately.

CHAPTER 20

———— ·❧·❧· ————

Sulking Is For Kids

Stop the sulking and start talking!
Validate each other's feelings without
being condescending or judgmental.
Grow up and have an adult conversation.

"WHAT'S WRONG?"

"Nothing."

"Was it something that I did?"

"You know what you did."

"Honey, if you don't tell me what I did, how can I fix it? Please talk to me."

If this sounds familiar, whether you're a man or woman, you know that having a partner who sulks instead of talking is frustrating. Sulking and pouting are not to be confused with a mutually agreed upon time out to give someone time to think things through by postponing the discussion. Postponement is often necessary for gathering thoughts and finding inner calm. Then when you're ready, you're better prepared to convey feelings about the situation and have a more meaningful discussion.

Sulking, on the other hand, is an extremely prolonged silent treatment on the part of one person. It's considered immature, manipulative, and, when used to exert power over a mate, has the potential to become a form of emotional abuse in which no resolution is either sought or explained.

To shed light on the subject of sulking is to better understand the subconscious mind. It is worthwhile to remember that the subconscious mind does not know the truth from a lie. Up until the age of seven, the subconscious mind is primarily programmed by caretakers and accepts whatever it downloads. This means that, if a person was allowed to sulk or pout as a child, the behavior is already imbedded into the subconscious mind. This is a simple explanation for a complicated behavior. When a person takes ownership of being a sulker and wants to change, he or she can learn to pause in order to gain insight into the customary pattern. A change of perception is important to understanding what really happened to trigger the sulking response.

Imagine this as a bright flashing Neon green sign: *Sulking is nongender.*

Repairing an established pattern of sulking requires rewiring the subconscious mind with new programming. This is done through awareness and repetition by the conscious mind until a new and improved program is formed with acceptable behaviors. So, just how is this rewiring done?

As soon as sulking appears in the relationship, it needs to be nipped in the bud through the implementation of these suggestions:

- Do not stoop to retaliation by sulking. The sulker is a master manipulator who is guaranteed to outlast his or her opponent. The only thing this sort of retaliation accomplishes is to keep the toxic cycle playing over and over and over, gaining strength each time.

- Do not apologize to a sulker a gazillion times. If you feel that you need to apologize, do so three times for it to be accepted. No more. Apologizing more than three times only gives the sulker more control and reinforces additional toxic behavior.

- Do not respond to the sulker by making angry threats; this type of response feeds fuel to the sulker. Rather, speak with an assertive yet soft, calm voice: "I can't resolve this problem by myself. I need for you to speak to me."

- As you deal with a sulker, do stay calm as you go about your day by doing something positive for yourself. Call someone (*not* to complain), go to the movies, read, or take a walk. Make sure to cook a delicious meal for yourself. At the same time, challenging as it is, refrain from letting his or her childish behaviors get under your skin. Speak as calmly as you can. "Would you like a sandwich?" "Care for a cup of tea?" If you don't get an answer, smile and make one for yourself.

Again, realize that there's a difference between sulking and taking time to cool off. Sometimes a person can make a rude or careless comment without realizing that there are going to be hurt feelings. At times like this, he or she just needs time to get in control and shake off any insults by using an "I" statement; for example, "I need time to process what you just said." When an "I" statement is used with your own words, your partner knows you'll be back within a reasonable amount of time to talk about the problem and reach a forgiving resolution. Sulking and using the silent treatment, on the other hand, can last for days, often leaving the partner feeling angry, frustrated, and resentful.

If a sulker isn't able to get out of sulking repeatedly through self-discipline, professional help is often needed for the sulker to self-evaluate. What caused the sulking in the first place? How effective are his or her communication skills? Is he able to honestly tell her how he feels? Is she able to genuinely listen to his concerns? A skilled therapist is able get to the underlying cause of the behavior with compassion and understanding. Balance is then restored to the relationship.

There are couples who practice telling it like it is from their own perceptions at the beginning of the relationship. When the husband does or says something embarrassing, she tells him about it. When the wife does or says something he doesn't like, he tells her. After seeing things through each other's eyes, they're able to apologize, let it go, and immediately move on.

So, put on your big-girl panties or your big-boy boxers, stop sulking, and start talking! It's time to grow up and communicate your true feelings in an honest, sincere, and mature voice.

CHAPTER 21

"I" Statement Communication

To communicate effectively, use your "I" statements.
When in doubt, ask questions.
Repeat to clarify what you think you heard.
Pay attention to body language.
Don't be mean. Keep it clean.

TRYING TO UNDERSTAND COMMUNICATION IN relationships can be equated with unraveling the secrets of the Universe. Verbal and nonverbal positive communication requires mindful practice. One way to acquire awareness of communication styles is to take an honest inventory of how people communicated growing up within your family unit. The way a child learns to communicate is usually by modeling adult behaviors.

For example, if a spouse has been bullied by a parent, caretaker, or teacher, he or she may have a tendency to shut down when communicating with a partner. This person may take years to find the confidence to open up and trust that it's okay to offer a different point of view.

Adults in another person's life may have been quick to anger and even to argue in front of kids, company, and the in-laws. This child may have been told mean and hurtful things. Minutes later, this same adult may have been laughing and joking and behaving as though nothing has happened. If an adult child acquires the same behavior patterns, his or her spouse may become confused and resentful at the inconsistent behaviors.

What about the adult child who had a parent with a closed mind—a "This is who I am so deal with it" kind of mentality? Hopefully, he or she will seek out a partner who is willing to be open to new ideas.

There's the withdrawn parent, the overly protective parent, the permissive parent, and the philosophical parent. Each has a personal style of resolving conflict. Study your own family structure and the arguing methods of your parents to see if you're able to find a match in your behaviors that support the same style. If you've already done that, you're a step ahead in figuring out your communication style and how to improve it.

Words matter. Communication matters. By examining your own history and methods of communication, in an objective, unbiased, non-judgmental way as possible, you will be able to make conscious minded improvements.

One technique that has been tried and true is using "I" statements. With these statements, you take ownership of your feelings without putting the listener on the defense. "You" statements—the ones usually used during an argument—gives the listener the impression that the speaker has control over his or her feelings. "You" statements are often interpreted as placing blame.

"I" statements take practice: "I feel frustrated when you don't call because I worry that something happened to you." In this sample, you are stating how you feel, and why. When you offer the reason that you feel the way you do, it serves as a legitimate explanation. It's a way of being assertive without putting the listener on the defense.

Now, let's review what a "you" statement looks like: "You make me so mad when you don't call!" Since you didn't give any explanation as to why it's important for him to call, it sounds as though you're blaming him for your anger, which means that you're giving him control over your emotions,

Here is a basic "I" statement template: I feel _____ when _____ because _____.

For example: "I feel *frustrated* when *I don't hear from you* because *I'm worried* something bad happened." In this sample, no blame or judgment is offered, and dialogue is kept open. Be careful to always follow "I feel" with an emotion like frustrated, hurt, scared, glad, sad, relieved, and so forth. "I" statements should be used to express joyful times as well as disappointments; for example, "I feel *loved* when *you rub my back* because *I know that you care.*"

Avoid saying "I feel *you* ____" statements. The word *you* immediately puts the other person on the defense. Another recommendation is to repeat what you hear in order to clarify what you think is being said. Ask for repetition or confirm your understanding: "Are you saying _____?" "I think what I hear you say is _____"

By restating what you hear, your partner has the opportunity to respond, "No, that's not what I meant at all. Let me rephrase that." Once both of you have restated and clarified respective perceptions of what was being said, you both have the satisfaction of being heard and understood. "What I meant was _____"

A large part of communication is being able to recognize the difference between hearing and listening. The ears never shut down. Even while sleeping, you're able to hear a bird tweet or a fire engine siren. So, while you may be hearing another person's point of view, it's important to stay nonjudgmental and listen to a reasonable explanation. Listening requires the use of eyes as you search for nonverbal cues.

Once all distractions have been removed and concerns are met with an open mind, your partner will know that you've listened with undivided attention; he or she will walk away with a sense of honestly being heard. Even though you may not necessarily change another person's opinion, it's okay, as long as seeds are planted for something to think about.

Follow these communication rules for a healthy marriage:

- Stay focused.

- Keep on track with the present problem.

- Never resort to name-calling, eye rolling, personal digs, or sarcasm.

- Speak calmly. How well can you listen if someone is shouting at you?

- Seek resolution. Release the need to be right or have the last word.

Couples love. Couples talk. Couples argue. Those are things that couples do.

Couples who know how to support each other and communicate with respect have stronger bonds. Words *do* matter.

PART 4

Mindful Infrastructure

Mindful infrastructure is crucial for understanding the delicate issues in an enduring relationship. In marriage, the five basic truths are obvious and simple:

1. Forgive past transgressions and be the hero of your story.

2. Be faithful in all areas of your life.

3. Respect each other at all times.

4. Trust that intentions are for one another's greater good.

5. Set boundaries of outside influences.

The truth is that healing begins with forgiveness, whether it's forgiveness or self or someone else.

The truth is that respect comes from being mature and releasing childhood fantasies of love.

The truth is that infidelity should never happen.

The truth is that trust is based on faith in one another.

The truth is that setting boundaries is easy, while holding a boundary is tough.

When ownership of these truths integrates with what you *know* in the depths of your soul to be honest, you're sure to find the reflection of happiness in all areas of your life. While doing the right thing may not be popular with friends, culture, or society, as my dad would say, "Doing what's right is never wrong."

CHAPTER 22

Forgiveness Is Freedom

Forgiveness improves physical health,
mental well-being, and emotional healing.
Forgiveness restores peace to your soul.
Forgiveness releases the victim and
makes you the hero of your story.
Forgiveness is for you.

"THAT'S UNFORGIVEABLE!" "I'LL NEVER FORGIVE you!" are phrases are common responses when reality confirms the pain of the unimaginable.

"I've said the words, but how will I know if I've really forgiven someone?" This is a question many have asked me. The short answer is, "You'll know." The long answer is, "When you're able to talk about your experience or tell your story without being emotionally attached to the gritty details. It's when you're no longer the victim and you're able to tell your story from the perception of being the hero because you *are* the hero. Once you've released attachment to the story, telling it will be like talking about a book you've read or a movie you've seen without emotional investment. When the heaviness of carrying the burden of anger and sorrow in your heart is released, the spirit automatically replaces it with the feeling of lightness and freedom. It is then that you'll know you have truly forgiven."

Whatever happened to you, today or seventy years ago, the past is the past. As horrifying as it was, and as imbedded as it is in the subconscious mind, it's time to release the pain and become the hero of your story. To understand forgiveness is to make a personal choice. You can choose to hold onto your anger and misery, or you can choose the path to physical and emotional freedom. Forgiveness provides the truth for unconditional love.

You may have heard someone make statements like these: "I've tried to forgive, but nothing happens." Or "I've tried to forgive, but I'm still angry."

All those hurts become stuck in the subconscious mind, simmering in past pain while gaining negative emotional strength every time you repeat your story. The bottom line is to stop telling your story. Just stop. Stop beating up your body with emotional pain. The time to forgive is now. Not tomorrow or next week. Now---this moment in time. Stop giving energy to past hurts. Release. Delete. Let Go. *Now!*

As a couple, situations arise all the time when you're asked to forgive yourself or your partner for any number of reasons: financial irresponsibility, a broken promise, unfulfilled expectations, or emotional trauma. Forgiveness doesn't mean you forget what happened to you. After all, those are learning lessons not to be repeated. Forgiveness means that as you release the power held over you by another person's words or actions, you're able to move on with greater inner strength, no longer a victim.

Forgiveness is a direct link to overwhelming health benefits. For example, holding onto anger in the long term is harmful to the body, often leading to physical ailments. The myth of being an unforgiving, tough person is just that—a myth. In other words, it takes a person of great strength to forgive. Holding onto emotional pain is an excuse to simmer in anger.

Here is the condensed version of what forgiveness looks like:

- Forgiveness does not mean that you need to tell the person who is being forgiven. Forgiveness is for you, not the other person. So, even if a person is deceased or already out of your life, you can still forgive in absentia.

- Forgiveness does not mean that you need to forget the experience. It happened. Only you can decide to be the hero of your story. Forgiveness releases the victim mentality.

- Forgiveness does not mean that you have to reconcile with the person who hurt you. The misperception about reconciliation may be one of the biggest fallacies of forgiveness. If someone has hurt you, you do not need to go back to repeat the pattern. Get the professional help that you need to move on.

- Forgiveness does not mean that you stay in an abusive relationship. No way! Stop repeating abusive patterns. Get the help that you need and cut ties with abuse now.

- Forgiveness does mean you must take ownership of your feelings and be accountable for your actions. Remember to forgive yourself for your own misperceptions.

- Forgiveness does mean that you take back your power by releasing a victim attitude and become the hero of your story. Give up the victim mentality and stop telling your story.

- Forgiveness does mean that it's time for you to find inner peace. It's amazing the lightness felt within once the pain is released.

- Forgiveness does mean that you legally seek justice and/ or compensation. Don't be manipulated into thinking otherwise. Seeking justice feeds an internal sense of fairness.

The important thing to remember about forgiveness is that, once your heart is open and released from pain, you're free to make clear decisions. Clear decisions lead to positive choices for moving forward. As you move forward, you're able to reach your full potential.

What about the unintentional hurt? It's hard to imagine that there's not one person who hasn't carelessly hurt someone's feelings. No one's perfect, so consider the intention when your loved one says or does something that you thought was hurtful or inappropriate. Put yourself in his or her shoes and ask yourself how circumstances could have been different. Has your perception shifted? Have you viewed the incident from the point of compassion? As long as it's not a consistent pattern of unkindness, choose wisely and acknowledge that everyone makes mistakes—even you.

If you're still stuck with anger, imagine a happier time in your life when you shared laughter and picturesque memories. Even if it's only one event, by shifting the perception of resentment to one of compassion and understanding, you will be able to release forgiveness and replace the anger with inner peace.

Once you've forgiven, the anger and bitterness leave, opening the spaces in your heart to be filled with fresh, amazing memories. When forgiveness replaces the negative feelings of resentment, guilt, and shame, be prepared for other relationships in your life to miraculously fall into place.

Being able to forgive whatever happened to you in the past is the most powerful gift you can give to yourself, and your partner, for physical, mental, and emotional health. For spiritual growth, forgiveness is like releasing sandbags from the basket of a hot air balloon. As the heavy sandbags of anger, guilt, and resentment fall away, you're able to float up, reach your full potential, and fill your spirit with love.

As soon as you make the decision to forgive, you've taken the first step to becoming the true hero of your story. I would be willing to bet that you can name someone right now who has overcome great obstacles of emotional pain whom you consider to be a hero, whether it's a character in a movie or someone you know in real life. Forgiveness is the one thing that can set you free to travel the path to unconditional love and enhance your spiritual journey.

CHAPTER 23

———— ·❧·❧· ————

Infidelity Hurts

Infidelity is never the answer.
Once the foundation of trust is broken,
it may never be restored.
Infidelity hurts.

INFIDELITY HURTS. PLAIN AND SIMPLE.

"How could I not have known?" Spouses ask this question after an affair has been unmasked. The injured party usually is embarrassed, feels stupid for believing the cover-up lies, and yet shocked at being blindsided with the truth.

Infidelity hurts. Just because the wounds aren't visible doesn't mean that the scars aren't there. If there are children, they should never feel that pain because it could linger and influence their relationships for the rest of their lives. Sure, children may say they are okay and put on a brave face for the world to see, but no one knows how children internalize pain, and depending on their age of understanding, in the end, they may foolishly end up blaming themselves.

It doesn't matter who chased whom, who got drunk and didn't know what he or she was doing. "I don't know how it happened!" doesn't cut it either, because it never, ever "just happens." Don't disrespect yourself with a string of "if only" excuses: "If only my parents had ...," "If only my job was ...," "If only my wife ...," If only my husband ...."

There are ethical differences in defining infidelity. Some people think that internet infidelity counts and some people think that, if there's no physical contact, a relationship doesn't exist. Only you can know the answer to when you've been unfaithful. A simple way to check your moral code is to ask yourself, "How would I feel if my spouse were to behave the same way I am?"

Not all marriages will last forever. Sometimes divorce *is* the best option for all concerned---that's a personal decision that, hopefully, you will never have to make. If you should determine that you no longer want to be married, make the decision in a way that will give you a clear knowing in your heart and in the deepest recesses of your soul that you did all that you possibly could have done to rekindle your love.

To anyone who is even *thinking* of having an affair, I strongly urge you to consider the consequences. I assure you, sooner or later, there are always consequences. Even if you and your spouse decide to stay together, once the foundation of trust is broken, there's a long road to restoring faith.

Fortunately, the majority of married couples are devoted and loving. Most spouses work on their marriages with united commitment to withstand the everyday stress of living in a complicated world.

As we live in a world of "what ifs" and "that depends," there may be morally acceptable exceptions. What if a partner is terminally ill and hooked up to tubes for an indefinite amount of time, considered to be severely mentally incapacitated, unable to function in today's world? What if church laws interfere? You must decide. No judgment.

As I stated that I would write this book in a positive voice, heed these words: I am *positive* that infidelity is not the answer to any problems.

CHAPTER 24

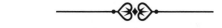

In-Laws Are Not Outlaws

*Set fair and mutually agreed upon
boundaries for in-laws.
Stand united and support each other.
Include in-laws, but don't open any door
that you don't want entered.*

WHILE IN-LAWS CAN BE PROBLEM solvers, joke tellers, sources of wisdoms, and loving huggers, they can also be meddling, conniving, and manipulative. Yes, in-laws can be angels on earth or as troublesome as ill-mannered trolls.

Couples who are dealing with the insensitive in-law or in-laws, beware.

I know about the devastating damage an in-law is capable of causing. Since I'm now a mother-in-law myself, I can well appreciate the weight and delicate balance of the role. Gratefully, I'm blessed to have a son-in-law and daughter-in-law who are thoughtful and kind, but not every parent is as lucky as I am.

There are some in-laws who may view your chosen partner as competition, and partners can also see in-laws as competition. Obviously, there's a huge difference between spousal love and parental love, but for an overly protective or controlling parent, that distinction may become muddled. To be clear, if you sense that there's jealously of any kind, talk about it openly and with compassion before it gets out of hand. Some parents just need to know that they're loved and not forgotten. In other words, if Mama Bear wants to continue to iron his jeans or Papa Bear wants to wash her car, are you going to be okay with that?

Most in-law problems are easily circumvented once reasonable boundaries are set at the outset. Calmly sit down with your partner and discuss a set of clear and concise boundaries that fit your family dynamics. If you need guidance, consult a counselor or an impartial third party. There can be no room for any misinterpretation when boundaries are presented to the in-laws. Don't assume anything! Remember, to assume is to make an "ass" out of "u" and "me."

Reasonable is the operative word. While it's true that what's reasonable for one couple may not be considered reasonable for another, make certain that common sense prevails. An easy way to test your boundaries is to put yourself in the in-laws' shoes. How would you feel with the same boundary? Is it a boundary you can adhere to?

Another way to maintain a positive relationship with family members is to pay close attention to what you say about your spouse when talking to your parents and siblings. Assuming they're rational, they already know couples have arguments, so no surprise there when one of you is in a dither and calls Mom or Dad for support. Keep in mind that, while you'll most likely forgive and forget, your in-laws may not. Some parents are understanding and able to see both sides of an issue and give solid advice, or at least recognize your need to vent and be an empathetic sounding board. On the other side of the spectrum, there are parents who may choose to hold onto whatever you tell them, stroke your anger, and become the undercurrent cause of name-calling and sarcastic remarks. Know which set of parents you have and act accordingly.

If you have a need to vent, make certain that, at other times, you tell the in-laws about all of the positive and thoughtful things that your partner does for you. It helps them to know that you may argue but you also solve disagreements through negotiation and compromise. No matter what, be loyal to your spouse by enforcing the agreed upon boundaries.

A rule of thumb is if the *wife* has an issue with *his* parents or extended family members, then *he* is the one who has to remind them about the boundaries. Conversely, if the *husband* has an issue with *her* parents or extended family, then *she* has to be the one to fix it with her family. To avoid the simmering pot of ill feelings, each of you needs to address issues diplomatically and as soon as a problem arises. Watchwords here are *quickly* and *calmly*. It's imperative not to permit problems to escalate.

A word of caution: Don't allow yourself to be coerced into doing something you don't really want to do. Don't let your words be twisted so they mean something different from the idea you intended. Be forgiving, not manipulated.

Realize that parents may not understand your boundaries so you may have to explain them more than once. Be prepared to answer questions. At the beginning, parents may need gentle reminders that you love them and that you want to include them in your life. Ask them to reminisce about memories of how they felt when they were first married. Maybe they've forgotten what it felt like to start a new life as one member of a two-member unit. Boundaries must be set according to your schedule and limits. If anyone messes up, move forward with a positive attitude and leave the past in the past.

So, what do you do when you have an in-law who repeatedly ignores boundaries? Stand firm and don't let anyone make you feel guilty. Use a serious tone of voice. Stay calm and strong. Whatever it takes, don't let anyone push your buttons or make you feel guilty. By the same standard, be careful not to resort to yelling, making demeaning comments, or acting in an unreasonable or crude manner.

If a parent disrespects your partner by making insulting innuendos, calling names, or making snide comments, leave the premises immediately. If you're talking on the phone and unkind comments are made, tell Mum or Dad that the boundary, which you've already thoroughly explained, has been crossed and you'll speak another time. Say good-bye and calmly hang up. Whether you live locally or hours away, leave. You can return after the in-law knows that you will not tolerate any verbal insults. Keep visits to a minimum until he or she knows that every time there's an insult, you will leave.

Holding boundaries isn't easy, because it's complicated. Holding boundaries isn't fun, because it's serious. But consistency is a necessary must-do in order to alter the negative behavior. Hopefully, the in-law who refuses to respect boundaries will be a quick learner.[3]

It's important to set reasonable boundaries ahead of time and not make them up as you go. Remain firm and consistent. Keep in mind, though, that once you break a boundary and decide to invite your in-laws into your lives, there are no takeaways. It would be like giving a kid a set of drums and getting mad at him for banging on them.

---

[3] In cases where drug or alcohol abuse, physical or mental abuse, or neglect are suspected, it is mandatory to get necessary help. If abuse of any kind *is* involved, protecting loved ones, particularly children, takes priority.

There are many times when you'll want all family members on board and involved. If an in-law is in real estate, it may be wise to listen to his experience when buying a house; if there's a doctor in the family, she may be the go-to person when health issues arise; if an in-law is a world traveler, he can provide vacation tips. Each family member has talents to share, so take advantage of them. When making your boundaries, keep these special gifts in mind.

It's great to include everyone in joyous events like holidays, birthday parties, recitals, sports events, award ceremonies, and so forth. Sometimes, new family traditions are created and in-laws need to be understanding and flexible. Be patient and give families time to adjust. Mom may not be ready to hand over the Thanksgiving turkey. And yet, you shouldn't be expected to eat two dinners just to make her happy.

Hopefully, you have in-laws who are supportive, nurturing, and understanding. But if you don't, and you end up with an in-law who is a meddling, mean-spirited troublemaker, maintain your personal dignity and show respect and courtesy for the parent of the awesome person you love. While making sure your loyalty remains with your partner, remember, you may be an in-law yourself someday.

CHAPTER 25

————— ·❦·❦· —————

Respect Is the Golden Rule of Marriage

Respect and treat each other
as you want to be treated.
Respect each other in every thought, word, and action.

MAN OR WOMAN, SHORT OR tall, jewels or tatters, mutual respect is a must in any relationship worth having. Without respect, nothing else works. *Respect* is a seven-letter word packaged with value and balance, neatly wrapped with common sense, decorated with the Golden Rule of Marriage: Respect and treat each other as you want to be treated.

Where respect for personal privacy is concerned, what dreams, fantasies, emails, checking accounts, and personal bathroom space needs to be respected? Would you want him to brush his teeth while you're taking a crap? When there are particular boundaries in question, respectfully discuss and resolve.

In a respectful relationship, you can still be true to yourself while carefully choosing your words, actions, and behaviors. An aspect of respect is being able to recognize the balance of power in your relationship and being mindful not to ever take advantage of any weaknesses or fears.

Respect is an act of being selfless, showing consideration, and standing by your partner through thick and thin. When you put him first, when you're supportive against the odds, when you're there for her, even if she doesn't ask—that's respect.

Eva was in charge of the costumes for the local community playhouse. Her husband, David, was the director of the play. I happened to be visiting when David received a phone call questioning the design of the costumes. David turned to Eva and asked, "What do you think about the costume design?"

Eva said, "I like them. Do you want to see one? I could show you."

He said, "No, that's okay. I don't need to see one. If you like them, that's good enough for me." And that was that.

While you'll still have disagreements, when there's respect, you'll know that your voice will be heard, your opinion will matter, your ideas will be shared, negotiations will be fair, and compromises will be equitable.

Judy writes about her forty-eight year marriage: "The thing that has held us together through the toughest of times is mutual respect. Life is challenging—no doubt! But when things have been really hard, I remind myself that if I didn't have his towel to hang up on the rack, I would miss it. When this whole thing started, I knew that he was mine. I still do. I felt then that I couldn't love him any more than I did. We have a history together, but that feeling of love and deep respect has never changed."

Respect is an inner confidence that your love is faithful and true. Once you're mindful of the need for mutual respect in your daily life, your marriage is more sure-footed on the path to long-lasting happiness.

CHAPTER 26

Trust in Love

Trust is a crucial element
when building the foundation of marriage.
Loving with full integrity builds trust.

TRUST IS AN ESSENTIAL CORNERSTONE in any relationship, especially when it comes to marriage. As soon as "I do" floats past your lips, what you're really saying is "I trust you with my heart."

In studying vibrational energy and mindfulness, I found that trust has a high vibrational frequency, to be accepted in full faith. When there is trust, the power of God flows through you, binding your love.

A trusting partner knows that confidences are to be kept private, safe and secure in your love. Trust offers sincere encouragement and values the sacred bond of marriage, regardless of any person, place, circumstance, or event. Trust transcends time and space.

In the home of trust, there is no room for jealousy, envy, or deceit. Once trust is shattered, can a saddened heart ever be restored? With each broken promise or unkind action, a nick is forever branded on the heart, as if a dull ax is attempting to chop down a mighty oak. The ax may not succeed, but the wounds and scars will remain on the tree.

Trust in each other with full faith in the freedom of your hearts, knowing your marriage is always going to be loving, caring, and true. Trust the honesty of handling the finances, trust the promise of your word, and trust the depth of your love.

Trust is being honest with yourself and the people in your life. Lies are intentional. Tell the truth even if it hurts, regardless if you know that it's something that she doesn't want to hear. Telling lies usually comes back to bite you in the butt much worse than if you had told the truth in the first place. So if the red dress really does make her look fat, tell the truth in a delicate, tactful way. "Honey, I think the black dress is sexier."

Trust is caring in thought, word, and deed, no matter where you are or who you're with. Trust is being true to the integrity of your word, ever faithful to never give into temptation. As one wife aptly said, "Trust is everything!"

The gift of trusting in love says, "I trust you with my heart. I trust the honesty of your word. I trust that you will care for me all of our days. With your love, I trust that I don't have to be strong all of time. I trust in the oneness of us."

PART 5
Mindful Money

Money plays a valuable role in every segment of life. One could even say that managing money is akin to being a maestro, masterfully directing every dollar to bring harmony into the home.

There are current teachings to suggest that, in order to attract more money, we must think positive thoughts and release any negative connotations, old sayings, and beliefs. Practice saying positive affirmations, and more money will come! The only challenge is that you have to say these mantras until your words become fully integrated into your subconscious belief system. In the meantime, while you work on changing your subconscious thoughts, concentrate on managing what you have in the here and now.

Since money drives the economy, it commands your household budget as well. No matter how much money is brought into the home, every household member needs to take responsibility for spending it wisely.

Jointly handling money can be a confusing process for many newlyweds. Living within a budget is like walking a tightrope; it's a delicate balance between spending and saving while meeting the family's needs. To be the best maestro for managing your money, take the time to learn the basic ins and outs of the financial world of credit cards; a little knowledge about interest rates can keep you from incurring insurmountable debt. In the long run, you'll be grateful that you did. May common sense prevail!

CHAPTER 27

———— ⊰⊱ ————

Finances Take Compromise

Value your financial stability.
Be realistic about your spending habits,
and prepare for the unexpected.
Budget, budget, budget!

FINANCES CAN BE A TOUCHY subject—difficult to talk about. It's actually considered one of the most uncomfortable conversations most couples ever have. Did you know that there are some couples who avoid the discussion of money until after they're married? The American Psychological Association states that money matters are the biggest contributor to family arguments and that handling finances is a "significant source of stress." (Bethune 2015, 38).

The fact is, everyone spends money; it's just a different process for each person. While one of you may want to splurge on shoes or clothes, your partner may prefer a new sound system or big-screen TV. Where one couple spends money on a huge mortgage payment, another family lives frugally all year to fund vacations or travel. Hobbies, clubs, activities, family celebrations, charities, vacations, and retirement funds are all things that need to be discussed and budgeted. If there are children, then additional expenses need to be considered.

Once two incomes are joined by matrimony, it's only natural to expect changes in how the money is spent. In many couples, one person usually handles paying the bills while major spending decisions are made together. The cost of living goes up every year, so couples need to be open about income, spending habits, and debt.

Many couples have the challenge of blending incomes along with spending styles. Where there are conflicting spending habits, it's important to keep the lines of communication open until a compromising solution is found.

One technique to finding a compromise is for each of you to write down a list of things that are most important to you with regard to how income should be spent. Compare your lists and discuss them. When you find things that overlap, put them first on your combined priority list. The rest are up for negotiation. During discussions, keep focused on reaching your agreed goals, *not* attacking your partner's spending tendencies.

To ensure each of you feels independent and valued, make certain to make allowances in your budget for pocket money that doesn't have to be accounted for. Whether couples decide on having joint or separate checking accounts, planning on how to blend incomes becomes a necessity. Some couples have three checking accounts: his, hers, and ours. In order to protect your money in case of an emergency, make provisions to access these accounts, such as adding your spouse's name or power of attorney.

Jeff and Chris agree: "Treat your relationship as though you're running a business. Respect your partner. Keep finances separate but pay mutual bills together. Whatever independent purchase you want is okay no matter what it is. Together purchases, like things for the house, are discussed and worked out."

The following is a sample of a basic budget form that I use. Once you see monthly bills written down, it'll be easier to see where your money is going every paycheck.

1.Total Income
2.Monthly expenses
Rent /mortgage
Homeowners insurance
Heating /cooling
Water, sewage
Garbage
Car payment
Car insurance
Health insurance
Cable or paid TV
Student loan
Cell phone/ landline
Credit card
Internet
Hair
Medications
3. Savings goals
Retirement

Vacation
Gift giving
Emergencies
4. Basic necessities
Groceries/pet food
Car/gas
Clothing /shoes
5. Discretionary spending
Charities
Entertainment
Non-essential services: _____   _____ Car washes _____   _____ Lawn care

As overwhelming as it may seem, after you design a plan for how you want to budget your money, reaching financial goals becomes easier and more manageable. A budget enables you to breathe easier when bills roll in.

So, whether you're flush with funds or living paycheck to paycheck, figuring out your finances is somber business that requires teamwork and being realistic about expenses. *Budget* is the watchword that will help you to stay in financial harmony. A joint understanding and openness of the family finances is crucial to prevent anyone from saying, "I didn't know."

CHAPTER 28

———— ·❂·❂· ————

Final Wishes Are Forever

*Make a will to let all of your final
wishes be known.
A will offers peace of mind for you and your family
and spares your loved ones from additional
grief and stress during an emotional time.*

MAKING YOUR FINAL WISHES KNOWN while you're young
and healthy is not a prediction that anything bad is going to happen.
According to a Gallup Poll published in May 2016 only 44 percent of
Americans have made a last will and testament to legally make these
wishes known. And even less have made a living will. Are you one of
them? (Jones. 2016).

The fact is that not one person leaves this earth alive. Not one.
Although this is an indisputable fact, talking about death and dying
can be awkward. It's easy to understand how the young and healthy
fail to fully realize that accidents happen, illness exists, and a life

can be transformed in one split second. That's why it's always best to be prepared rather than to take the chance of leaving your family wondering what to do. At the same time, loved ones are protected from additional stress during an emotional crisis.

As each situation is different, a good place to start is by having an open dialogue about final wishes. What may begin as an uncomfortable conversation, with older parents especially, making decisions may actually offer solace and relief.

Topics of discussion include who will inherit your property. In a marriage, usually the surviving spouse automatically inherits, but check the laws of your state regarding inheritance tax.

Dying without a will is called dying intestate. In those cases, the laws of your resident state will determine how your property is distributed, and it may be a settlement that you do not like. If no relatives are found, the estate goes to the state. It's always best to make your intentions clear ahead of time. Don't assume anything!

The purpose of a last will and testament puts your mind at ease by establishing the following:

- Funeral arrangements, including: cremation or burial, where you want to be buried or what you want to have done with your ashes, church, type of service—memorial or gravesite—music, flowers, and other wishes

- Who will carry out your final wishes or be the executor of your will

- Organ donations

- Honors a "living will" specifying whom is to make medical treatment decisions in circumstances which you are no longer able to express informed consent

- Beneficiaries who will receive either special property or personal possessions: children, friends, businesses, charities, and other organizations

- Backup beneficiaries in case the ones named don't survive

- Person responsible for caring for your pets

Wills can be changed as needed by adding a codicil, an easier way to make amendments to a current will without having to rewrite the entire document. Nothing is permanent until the last will is the last will.

Regardless of how much money, property, or valuables you have, greed and avarice will always exist. Protect your loved ones legally by putting your final wishes in writing. It's an easily doable way to avoid family squabbles. Let it be known who inherits Grandma's handmade quilts or Grandpa's baseball card collection. Never assume. Get everything in writing. And I mean everything.

While it's best to meet with an estate planner or attorney, whatever you do, get something in writing and have it witnessed. Don't you think that it's better to be properly cared for and have your final wishes honored? Sad as it may sound, writing a will adds contentment to your life.

CHAPTER 29

————•⟨✦⟩•————

The Savings Plan

*Tuck away a predetermined
amount of money each payday.
Be mindful of your spending habits.
The time to save is now.*

LIFE PASSES BY AS QUICKLY as the spark of a thought. Speaking from the voice of experience, I know that the future will be here faster than you can say "retirement." The time to save is *now*.

Ever since the financial crisis of 2008, *caution* is the operative word when moving forward. Today, more than ever, it's important to have money tucked away for the unexpected; in fact, experts recommend putting away enough to cover up to six months of expenses. A rule of thumb suggests that 20 percent of monthly income should be saved for that proverbial rainy day.

I'm not a financial strategist, and I strongly urge you to do independent research into whatever financial service company you chose to use.

What I have found are a few basic bits of information that you may find useful.

- First, choose a certified financial advisor. Beware of the terms: financial analyst, financial advisor, financial consultant, investment counselor, and wealth manager as they are generic terms or job titles and may be used by investment professionals who may not hold any specific credential. Bottom line: seek a *certified* financial planner.

- Second, even if you find an advisor who is credentialed, you need to realize that he or she works on commission and may not offer advice necessarily in your best interest, but rather, based on how much commission to be made. For example, annuities, although good for some people, may not be the right investment for you. Annuities have hidden fees, and the financial advisor may be offered incentives to push them as investments. Although legal, is this someone you would want to handle your money?

- Third, search for an advisor who's a *fiduciary* to handle your financial matters. Fiduciary advisors are *legally* bound to act in your best interest.

- Fourth, find out if your employer offers a 401K retirement plan. However, watch out for a list of legally hidden fees that you're expected to pay—legal fees, trustee fees, participation fees, record-keeping fee, transactional fees, stewardship fees, bookkeeping fees, and so on. While your money is earning money, even with compound interest, these seemingly small fees can add up over time, losing you a substantial amount of money.

- Fifth, before you invest, check out low-fee index funds, which are funds that are groups of stocks that try to mirror a stock market index. There's also a higher-fee index fund for which investors pick the stocks for you. There are no guarantees, however, that they, or anyone else, can make accurate predictions in picking stocks. Low-fee index funds are considered passively managed funds to be checked on periodically.

- Sixth, consider becoming a member of a credit union. Although they are not for everyone, credit unions are nonprofit institutions that serve their members, not customers. Because credit unions are owned and operated by members, and insured by FDIC, your money is always safe. The National Credit Union Insurance Fund (NCUIF) reports, "Not one penny of insured savings has ever been lost by a member of a federally insured credit union." Credit unions also offer lower interest rates on loans. Credit unions differ in services offered, so check before making a decision. If you're not a risk taker, the credit union may be the right fit for you.

In a nutshell, to begin your savings plan:

1. Find a certified financial advisor

2. Find a financial advisor who is a fiduciary.

3. Find out if your employer offers a retirement plan.

4. Watch out for legally hidden fees in your retirement plan.

5. Check into switching from stocks to bonds.

6. Keep any fees under one percent.

7. Consider joining a credit union.

No one is suggesting that, as you save money for your future, you must walk around with holes in your shoes. Just be realistic when buying for your family's needs. Trust your instincts to know when you're spending too much. Do whatever is necessary to take control and rein yourself in. Before using your credit card, ask yourself, "Do I want it?" "Do I need it?" and "When can I pay it off?"

Practice the mantra, "*I choose* not to buy this now." You'll gain tremendous self-empowerment as *you* mindfully make the positive choice of not purchasing something. Saying "I can't afford it" implies that you don't have the power of choice and reinforces negative thoughts about money in the subconscious mind.

Avoid comparing your haves and have nots with those of your neighbors and friends. So what if the Jones's buy newer cars or go on exotic vacations? As a couple, you need to decide the best way to fulfill the necessities and desires to best serve your family.

One wife said, "My husband is one of the most easygoing men on the planet, but he still doesn't understand when I pay full price for something. He buys something only if it's on sale, or he doesn't buy it at all. He says that there isn't anything he wants badly enough to pay full price. In the end, we always compromise."

Are you living pay-to-pay as it is? Get a piggy bank and save your loose change, or save a dollar a day, which turns into thirty dollars a month. Before you know it, you will have saved $365 in one year! Instead of stopping for espresso on your way to work, add your coffee money to the till and take your own caffeine from home. Pack your own lunch. Use coupons. Watch for bargains. Carefully search for a low-interest credit card for emergencies.

Regardless of how you chose to save, make the decision today. When you and your partner are on the same page when it comes to saving, by sharing the same fiscal economic goals, you won't miss what you don't have, and saving money will soon become a reward in itself. Watch with enthusiasm as your account grows!

I've learned how tremendously important it is to pay close attention to your own retirement plan and not leave it entirely in the hands of someone else. By all means, ask questions. Educate yourself and stay on top of your investments.

I'm blessed to have been a teacher in Pennsylvania where my school district automatically deducted a certain amount out of my paycheck every month. During our struggling years, my husband would say that we needed that money. We did, but if the district hadn't forced me to save for retirement, I'm fairly certain that I would not have the secure income that I am grateful to have each and every day.

Even if you don't have a forced retirement plan, design one for yourself. As tempting as it may be to spend your money now, the day for retirement will soon be upon you. Visualize how you want to retire so that, when the time comes, you'll have an income to assure your peace of mind.

As Geoffrey Chaucer said, "Time and tide wait for no man."

CHAPTER 30

·❧·

Teamwork Gets the Job Done

Commitment + Compromise + Cooperation = Teamwork
Teamwork says, "We're on this ride together."

MEMBERS OF A HOUSEHOLD WITH one bathroom quickly learn about teamwork. Showering, brushing teeth, applying makeup, styling hair, and the morning constitution require the choreography that can be the envy of any dancer, especially when privacy concerns are factored into the equation.

Working as a team requires commitment, compromise, and cooperation.

The element of commitment reminds me of the coach who's committed to making the best team possible by recognizing and supporting each member's strengths and skills. Couples who make this same commitment recognize the individual needs of each family member and make choices for the stability and growth of the connected family unit.

Compromise is the art of give and take and meeting somewhere in the middle. If something really, really means a lot more to one partner and not so much to the other, the use of problem solving skills can make it a win-win team decision for both. Cooperation means relinquishing ego without any hidden agendas. Regardless of who makes more money, cooperation on the home front means that you work together by balancing responsibilities for the best possible outcome.

One consistent thread of teamwork is the importance of couples being able to share the same vision and goals. So when stuff happens, as it does in life, and detours have to be taken, in the end, you're still going in the same direction, staying in the flow.

Nicole said, "When I dated my husband, we had the same thoughts on God, love, and the Universe. Our opinions might differ on the small stuff, but we are always going in the same general direction. It's been very helpful. When the road gets bumpy, it's good to know that there isn't a different road you would rather be on."

Teamwork in a marriage is as necessary as climate stability for Earth. Your attitude, effort, and willingness to do whatever it takes for the betterment of your home will influence you and all future team members for the rest of your lives.

PART 6

Mindful Living

We hold these truths to be self-evident,
that all men are created equal,
that they are endowed by their Creator with
certain unalienable rights, that among these are
Life, Liberty and the pursuit of Happiness.
Declaration of Independence, 1776

Mindful living means making choices that enhance the dream of growing old in a lifetime of love. During your journey, take advantage of opportunities, feel the thrill of accomplishing the impossible, breathe with peace in your soul, lighten the load of others less fortunate, and leave a legacy of respect by living a life of honor and integrity.

What do you want to achieve on your path to living well? Are you willing to make a sincere commitment to create the life that fulfills your deepest desires?

Take nothing for granted and observe life with discerned perception. Ask yourself how you can reach your ultimate best and create your own love story with grace and gratitude.

At the end of the day, living well has nothing to do with the size of your house, how many cars you have, or the number of possessions that surround you. In your pursuit of happiness, choose to live your life guided by the grace of God, with tolerance, patience, and kindness to all.

Here is my father's philosophy for living a rich life:

Wherever You Go, There You Are

An old man peacefully rocked on the porch of an old-timer's rickety service station, lazily smoking a corncob pipe. The sign dangling from the front of the gas pump read: Last chance for gas before city limits.

Smoke from his pipe softly faded into the still air as a family pulled up for gas and a bit of advice. The old man moseyed over to the outdated gas pumps and slowly placed the nozzle into the tank. The numbers, even more slowly, flipped over, counting the gallons.

The father of the family impatiently tapped his foot as he restlessly looked about. He asked the old man, "What kind of town is up ahead? We're looking to resettle someplace, and I would like to know what we can expect from the people there."

"Well," the old man drawled, as he answered the question with a question: "What kind of town was your last one?"

"It was awful!" the man proclaimed. "Full of hateful, back-stabbing trouble makers!"

"Well," said the old man, again drawing out his words, "I think that is the same kind of town you'll find here."

The father hurriedly paid the old man, and, with his car wheels spinning and kicking up dust, he quickly spun his car around and headed in the opposite direction.

Before long, another family stopped for gas. They too were planning to resettle, and sought advice about the town. "What kind of town is up ahead? We're looking to resettle."

This time, the father of the family offered to help the old man when he noticed him walking with a limp and struggling with the old-fashioned gas pump nozzle.

The old man answered the question by asking the same question as he had before, "Well, what kind of town was your last one?"

As the father patiently helped the old man with the heavy nozzle, he answered in a calming voice, "Our town? It was wonderful! Everyone was kind and considerate, and we made many lifelong friends."

"Well," said the old man with a smile, "That's the same kind of town you'll find here. Welcome!"

CHAPTER 31

———◈·◈———

Atmosphere Sets the Vibrational Tone

Music, flowers, laughter, and living in grace
all contribute to an inviting
atmosphere of peace and harmony.

THE VIBRATIONAL TONE IN YOUR home is raised by love, sweet love, creating a sense of lightness while affecting every sense of your quantum being, including your health.

Have you ever been a member of a group in which there is that one person who is constantly complaining? Does the negativity affect your comfort level? As you look around the room, is everyone else sensing the awkwardness? Notice how this one negative person affects the entire group. Chances are, that person doesn't even realize how he or she is influencing the atmosphere of the room. When cynicism and intolerance are companions, the entire energy field is negatively affected. Be mindful of speaking with complaint or judgment.

Are you aware that how you speak to your partner affects the atmosphere of your home? Do you greet your partner with a hug or with criticism? Are your words for her filled with care and concern or coldness and indifference? Even if you both have swinging-door schedules, do you take the time for a *real* kiss before starting the day and ending the evening?

Raising the vibration of the atmosphere is literally as simple as pressing the "play" button on your MP3 player. Once music enters the scene, the energy of the room becomes electrified, whether it is calming the anxious mind, setting your toes to tapping, or enhancing the mood for passionate lovemaking. Let there be music!

Smell is another sense that plays a powerful role in creating a welcoming atmosphere. A bouquet of flowers brings beauty while its sweet fragrance pleases the senses. Essential oil diffusers add a pleasant mist of freshness, and the aroma of freshly baked cookies creates a warm, homey atmosphere.

Laughter creates a vibration that has always been a staple to increase the lightness of a home. Watching comedies; healthy joking around; telling humorous stories; or playing a board game, cards, or silly jokes all add to an uplifting atmosphere. Even a loving smile at your sweetie goes a long way to increase the vibrational tone of the home.

To feel less like ships passing in the night and more like ships following the beam of light to a safe harbor, make it a priority to preview the upcoming week's calendar of events, workload, and appointments. When it's written on a calendar, there's no need for "I already told you" or "I forgot." A hanging erasable white board calendar is inexpensive and easy to find. Weekly updates help keep everyone calm and informed. Planning ahead becomes easier. Where one erasable board is helpful, two are even better at keeping monthly events on track.

For an atmosphere full of grace, I'm not suggesting that you walk around with a goofy grin pasted on your face or allow the neighbor's kid to feel free to raid your refrigerator. Neither must you keep your home white-glove clean.

The atmosphere of living in grace says, "I care about what's happening in your life." Grace is shown through listening to everyday happenings. Grace offers kindness, encouragement, and patience with yourself and others.

Your home is your sanctuary. A mindful home is filled with love and joy and thoughtful consideration for one another. It provides a welcoming atmosphere to be admired.

CHAPTER 32

---·⟨⊰⊱⟩·---

Eat, Rest, and Be Merry

*A full tummy and a solid night's rest ensures your
partner's full attention for a meaningful conversation.*

MAN OR WOMAN, IT DOESN'T really matter—eating is physical
thing. Whenever hunger strikes, your blood sugar drops. When your
blood sugar drops, you become irritable. Just as the body requires fuel
for energy, the brain needs fuel to enhance clear thinking. To make
decisions with a clear mind, your stomach can't be growling so that all
you can think about is finding something to eat. Your brain and body
require nourishment. Think about it—aren't you the most mellow
after a fulfilling meal?

Also, how well can you possibly listen to or discuss matters of
importance when you're tired? No one can. When you are exhausted,
your brain basically shuts down, disabling the wiring for clear
thinking.

Children are our greatest teachers for insight into human behavior. If a child is crying, fussy, or isn't as pleasant as usual, a parent explains, "Oh, it's past his naptime. He's tired." Or, "She hasn't eaten yet. She's just hungry."

Have you ever tried to motivate a tired, hungry child? It simply isn't happening! How about trying to talk to a weary, hungry adult? It's not happening either!

Without proper food and rest, all human bodies react the same way. So, unless it's a pressing decision that demands an immediate resolution, even the hardiest of persons need to eat and rest. You can always reopen the discussion later. Schedule it on your erasable calendar.

CHAPTER 33

—— ·❦·❦· ——

Who's the Boss?

As lifelong partners, you share the same vision.
Although the skills and roles may be
different, each partner is equal.

WHO WEARS THE PANTS IN the family? This question is not heard very often these days, as the roles of couples have matured over time. While it no longer matters who brings home the bacon or does the cooking, what does matter is equal respect. As couples find balance in responsibilities, power, and individual talents, and no one is trying to overshadow the other, contentment and happiness are certain to ring true.

If you haven't received the memo that this is the age of "balance in marriage," then it's time to pay attention. Balance doesn't mean that you give up your individual hobbies and interests. It means you must be open for any type of discussion. You must take time to listen, find middle ground, and reach decisions like grown-ups are supposed to.

Lydia said, "I think one of the reasons our marriage works is that neither one of us is bossy or needs to be in control. Like I told my kids when they got married, once you begin your marriage by talking and listening to each other, it'll stay that way."

How a person is raised influences how he or she interacts as one half of a couple. Once behaviors are imbedded into the subconscious mind, only those who have insight and mindfulness are able make the choice to keep behaviors that are beneficial and discard the ones that aren't. No one person should be in control, making all of the decisions. For example, no one should have to stand in wait for a tight wallet to open for grocery money.

Set boundaries through thoughtful discussion at the onset of the relationship—like a teacher establishing classroom rules on the first day of school. Otherwise, insecurity, resentment, and guilt are bound to take hold. In time, as the human heart clings to all emotions, long-term stress and depression from fear, anger, grief, or shame may manifest in any number of ways, including health issues such as chronic pain.

If one spouse acts like a prideful peacock with a constant need to be in charge, the damage to the relationship can be compared to the administering of a slow drip of emotional poison until both parties are miserably unhappy and the desire for true intimacy is destroyed.

When spouses offer mutual respect, listen to each other's concerns, offer support, and talk to each other to seek equitable solutions, they find a healthy balance in marriage. Being married is a 24/7 commitment. I know that I've said it before, and I'll say it again: follow the Golden Rule of Marriage: Respect and treat each other as you want to be treated.

In all things, let there be balance. You're going to be spending a ton of time together, so you may as well be equally happy.

Joanne and Hank agree. Joanne says, "I think that our maturity at this point in our lives plays a role. We have little stress at this stage. We have equal incomes and the same spending habits. We make each other laugh at about almost everything. And there are lots of hugs and back rubs!" Hank adds, "We also have patience and gratitude!"

CHAPTER 34

────•❦•❧•────

Hugs Are Free

Hugs are free. Hugs are natural.
Hugs naturally produce the love hormone oxytocin.
Have you hugged your spouse today?

HUGS ARE AMAZING! PEOPLE HUG as a friendly greeting, to share happiness, and to offer comfort in times of sadness. It's amazing that something as simple as a hug can play so many different roles! And, the best part is that hugs are free!

Mind blowing as it is, hugs trigger the release of a natural hormone, oxytocin, which is one of the major happy chemicals. Located at the base of the brain is the hypothalamus, which produces oxytocin. Because oxytocin can be activated by "human touch," it is often referred to as the love hormone. It lowers the levels of stress, elevates moods, and even increases the tolerance for pain. Research shows that couples who are physically close have higher levels of oxytocin. Any and all physical contact, including hugs, snuggling, holding hands, and sitting close, affects oxytocin levels in a positive way.

This astonishing hormone is released by even something as simple as a handshake. In fact, all bodily contact has been proven to produce the oxytocin hormone when accompanied by thoughtful actions, like a back rub or foot massage. Oxytocin is considered an essential ingredient to maintaining a loving relationship.

Until hugs become a part of your daily routine, write "Have you hugged your spouse today?" on a sticky note and stick where you can see it every single day—car visor, bathroom mirror, refrigerator, or even the computer screen. Let this message be your personal billboard to remind you to hug your loved ones every day.

Psychotherapist Virginia Satir is known for saying that people need hugs for survival, maintenance, and emotional growth. So, go ahead and hug your sweetie! You'll be glad that you did.[4]

Coronavirus update: Stay safe and hug only close family members.

---

[4] Common sense and cultural acceptance has to comply. Ask permission first, especially for nonfamily members. Be respectful of others and considerate of the circumstances. Accept that it's okay if some people don't want a hug.

CHAPTER 35

───◈◆◈───

Lucky in Love

How lucky you are to have found
the love of your life!
Dedicate yourself to the journey and share your love story.

HOW LUCKY FOR YOU THAT you have found your true love in a sea of millions. While some call it luck, the Universe surely aligned the moon and stars to arrange for you both to be at the exact spot at the exact moment in time so you could meet.

Linda and Herb met while visiting at the hospital where both of their fathers shared a room after having heart attacks. "While our dads were sleeping, it was only natural for us to start talking. We found out that we had a lot in common and, after our dads were recovering at home, Herb called me for a date." The rest is history as they just celebrated their fiftieth wedding anniversary.

The story of how you met your lover is your personal chick-flick romantic movie. Every time you share your love story, the emotions attached to that meeting are reignited. Where there is love, luck will find a way.

Fred's blue eyes twinkle as he delights in telling the story of how he saw Jean across the school dance floor. She was in eighth grade. He was a senior. For him, it was love at first sight. "It was like a scene from a movie," Fred says. He remembers telling his friend, "I'm going to marry that girl." His friend laughed and told him to get real. Fred patiently waited until Jean graduated high school before asking her out. When they married, the doubtful friend was in their wedding party. They have been married for fifty-eight years, and they are still feeling lucky in love.

As soon as you welcome love into your heart, you cross into the threshold of trust. You trusted your heart to recognize the love the Universe sent to you in the disguise of being lucky. Now, it's up to you to hold the sacredness of that gift.

John is from Pittsburgh. Rose is from Pittsburgh. Yet their paths never crossed until they attended the same conference a thousand miles away. Now, going on seven years, they consider themselves to be lucky in love.

What is your perception of what is and isn't considered luck during the ups and downs throughout the years? I'm reminded of a folklore tale about a farmer who worked very hard in his fields.

The Farmer's Luck

One day, the horse of a hard-working farmer ran away. His neighbor quickly came to him and said, "What bad luck! I'm sorry that your horse ran away!"

"Bad luck or good luck?" says the farmer. "We'll see."

The next day, the horse returned, bringing a drove of wild horses with him. The neighbor returned, "How wonderful! What good luck you have! Look at your great fortune!"

The farmer replied, "Good luck or bad luck? We'll see."

The following day, the farmer's son was taming one of the wild horses. He was thrown from the horse and broke his leg. The neighbor again appeared with condolences. "What bad luck for your son to break his leg!"

Again the farmer replied, "Bad luck or good luck? We'll see."

Soon, an army came through the village taking every able-bodied young man to go and fight in a war, but the son was spared because of his broken leg.

So, the story goes on and on. Good luck or bad luck? Is there such a thing?

If you go through marriage thinking that the ups and downs are good or bad, think again. There's no way that you can control what happens. You can control only your perception and how you react. Think about your life and how something you first thought of as bad turned into something good.

In the story of the farmer, his neighbor's emotions swept the range of high to low every time something happened, while the farmer kept consistently steady and true without judgment.

Look for the good in the bad and the bad in the good, and your marriage is sure to be one of the lucky ones.

PART 7

Mindful Romance

The thought of romance brings to mind steamy love stories and chic-flick movies in which wit, bravery, and true love are sure to conquer the maiden's heart.

Keeping the spark alive in your relationship takes desire, willingness, and creativity. Romance is sensuous, passionate, and exciting! Through romantic gestures, you're certain to keep that fuzzy tingle in your tummy alive and glowing for years to come:

A cozy fire
A candlelit dinner
A couple's massage
Watching a sunset
A carriage ride
Candles
The sweet smell of lavender
Chocolate-covered cherries
A warm sudsy loofah bath
Soft, sexy music
Sexy jammies
A get-away weekend
A gentle kiss on the cheek
Flowers ... always flowers

~~~

All of these lead to romance.
Breathe deeply.   Love is in the air.

CHAPTER 36

———— ⋅◈⋅◈⋅ ————

Flirting Is a Silent Tango

A moment of silent flirting
will keep your relationship scintillating
and on simmer for a love that lasts forever and ever more.

FLIRTING IS A POWERFUL SILENT language that enlists the use of only your body and eyes to convey the message "I'm interested." The art of flirting comes naturally to most of us. When you first met your mate, you most likely tilted your head ever so slightly and casually tossed your hair or sensuously pursed your lips. Unconsciously, you adjusted your clothes, playfully twirled your drinking straw, and seductively finger played your necklace or earrings.

Flirting through touch sends silent messages. He ever-so-lightly touches her arm. Her hand slightly rests on his leg. She adjusts his necktie. He sucks in his stomach. All the while, both share a genuine teasing smile.

At a gathering, you share an inside joke with just a knowing look from across the room. An impulsive kiss, a quick wink, a slight pat on the behind, or a gentle squeeze of the shoulder sends the message "I think you're hot and can't wait to get you alone!"

It doesn't matter if you've been married for one day or for a million decades, the secret language of flirting continuously bonds you together with each knowing wink.

Flirting Is Forever

Blue-haired Virginia and silver-haired Fred had been married a gazillion years when I was their guest at a large family gathering.

Virginia was wearing a simple cotton printed housedress and was in a lively conversation with a group of women standing near an extensive Victorian wrap-around porch. Fred was standing at the railing. His mind seemed to be in another galaxy as his aged blue eyes wistfully watched Virginia.

Ever so quietly, I silently stood next to Fred, wondering what could have taken his thoughts so far away. I didn't have to wait long as he whispered, "Look at her—she's as beautiful now as she was the day we were married." He sighed, softening his shoulders, remembering the past.

As though on cue, Virginia raised her head and looked directly at Fred. She tilted her head slightly and flashed a warm smile and a quick wink before returning to her conversation. Fred grinned. Still flirting. Still in love.

Fred and Virginia taught me that, by flirting, you'll always be a moonstruck lad or a lighthearted lassie, lovingly pierced by Cupid's arrow.

CHAPTER 37

———◆———

I Love You More

Never let a day go by without telling your loved one,
"I Love You."
Daily reminders of love and affection will
warm your hearts and lift your spirits.
"I love you" are three little words that
make the world go round.
I love you ... with all my heart.
I love you ... unconditionally.
I love you ... to share my life's adventure.
I love you ... with full commitment.
I love you ... completely.
I love you ... and adore you.
I love you ... now, forever, and evermore.
I love you ... more than you'll ever know.
I love you ... and all your body parts.
I love you ... more than pizza, sports, and back rubs.
I love you.
I love you.

FACT: IT TAKES LESS THAN two seconds to say, "I love you." In fact, it takes 1.24 seconds by my stopwatch—1.24 seconds to lift the spirits of the person you love.

Simply by hearing "I love you," she'll always feel cherished. He'll know that you deeply care. Value these magical words spoken from a sincere heart.

Melissa says that for her, marriage is "Unconditional love. Deep love. The only way to be able to truly accept your partner and not be bothered about what he does and doesn't do is to love each other deeply and unconditionally."

Say "I love you" to your parents, children, friends, and always to the one person in the world who lights your life and keeps the flame alive. Taking out the dog, making a fresh pot of coffee, or covering her when she falls asleep on the couch are all ways to say, "I love you."

CHAPTER 38

---◆❧◆---

Kissing Is More Than a Kiss

*Kissing releases pain and replaces it with pleasure
while bonding the relationship. Kiss your partner in
the morning, in the evening, and anytime in between.*

"TARZAN AND JANE UP IN a tree, K-I-S-S-I-N-G. First comes love, then comes marriage, then comes Jane with a baby carriage!" This was one of my favorite jump rope rhymes when I was a kid, and we substituted names as crushes changed with each year. As I got older, spin the bottle was the kissing game of choice. And the bottleneck would always land on the "wrong" boy. Even though it was only a quick kiss, it still counted. When it comes to adult love, marriage, and a baby carriage, kissing is an enchanting way to embrace your love.

Kissing as lovers creates great intimacy. I don't mean the kind of social kisses I share when I meet my friends and we greet each other with tight-lipped pecks to the cheeks. Sensual kisses are gentle kisses on the lips, earlobes, neck, tip of the nose, forehead, shoulder, the inside of your wrist, or other body parts. These kisses signal a deep desire for foreplay and passionate sex.

Of course, not all kissing leads to the bedroom. As couples are heading out the door in different directions on any hectic morning, a kiss goodbye sends the message that says, "I'll be thinking of you today." And when you come home at the end of the day, a welcome-home kiss says, "I'm grateful to have you to come home to." Kissing is a way to strengthen your love, relieve the stress of the day, and reignite the sparks of romance.

There are some fantastic scientific tidbits about what happens as lips unite in blissful pleasure:

- The happy chemicals, dopamine and oxytocin, deliver a sensual, physical message that speed travels through an intense array of nerves.

- The brain receives the signal that senses emotional bonding.

- Stress is relieved.

- Metabolism is boosted.

- The basic foundation of a committed, intimate, and romantic connection is reinforced.

- Men can live up to five years longer if they kiss their wives every morning.

So when the occasional headache emerges, a kiss, with all the happy healing neurotransmitters released, may just be the answer.

To keep your love afloat, kiss your partner passionately, softly, and with tantalizing enthusiasm. No matter the age or physical limitations, a kiss is still a kiss.

CHAPTER 39

——— ❖ ———

Wellness Pampering Is a Gift of Love

Pamper each other with care and tenderness every day.
To show that you care, think of ways
to do wellness pampering.

HAVING GRAPES HAND FED TO you as if you are a Grecian goddess is totally cool, but in the real world, most people would be grateful for a hot cup of tea even when they are not sick. Wellness pampering is what it implies—being pampered while you're healthy enough to fully appreciate it. Here are just a few wellness pampering ideas for both of you:

Attend an activity or event without complaint.
Pamper tired feet with lotion.
Give a neck, shoulder, or back rub.
Give spontaneous hugs.
Kiss her as you pass her chair.
Listen when he speaks.
Meditate together.

Leave love notes.
Plan a spa visit.
Tell her that you love her ...
... for absolutely no reason at all.

When pampering is done from the place of "just because" love instead of necessity, it becomes even more appealing, gratifying, and sensual to the receiver. When all is said and done, pampering refreshes the fluttering butterflies in your gut that you first had when you knew that you were in love with this amazing person.

Be creative with the ways you pamper. Whether it's a back rub or planning spa time together, everyone enjoys a little wellness pampering.

CHAPTER 40

———— ·❧·❦· ————

Be Playful and Touch the Sky

Release the kid inside and play with a happy heart.
Be creative, playful, and have fun!

REMEMBER THOSE DAYS OF PLAYGROUND fun as a kid? The harder you pumped the swing, the higher you flew until you felt that you could touch the sky! When there is playfulness woven through the fabric of the solemn tone of marriage, staying in love is cemented with that same contagious sound of laughter.

Some people are more natural at releasing inhibitions, acting silly and childlike, and not taking every little thing personally. Others need to be coaxed a little more.

Grownups with playful attitudes possess total disregard for being judged or criticized.[5]

---

[5] Playfulness never includes any activity that is lewd, crude, or loud. These elements can lead to embarrassment.

I recall attending a summer street fair where there was a couple dancing in the middle of the road. Their energy was magnetic, and it was mirrored in the smiling faces gathered around to watch. It was like being lured into a bakery, but instead of the fragrance of fresh baked bread, the crowd was drawn into the liveliness and energy of the enchanting couple.

In the private recesses of the boudoir, playful couples share intimate moments as giggles of lighthearted laughter dominate the scene. Whether it's chocolate, whipped cream, ice cubes, costumes, or a stripper's pole, enjoy whatever you have on hand. When an opportunity for spontaneous whoopee shows up enjoy one another with lighthearted optimism.[6]

Imagine an invisible energy field, approximately an arms width around you. It is known as your aura. Whenever you act joyfully, this energy field radiates happiness like bees spreading pollen in the springtime. Friends feel comfortable and relaxed, and strangers smile without even knowing why, thanks to your positive vibe.

When asked for their formula for a happy marriage, David said, "I think it's important that we share the same world views." Eva agreed, adding, "We also dance and have fun playing together!" David laughed. "Yes! We certainly do have fun." Keeping the home fires burning with playfulness is like sliding down a waterslide—the twists and turns end with a splash of fun. Go ahead and touch the sky!

---

[6] Write suggestions of wild abandon on strips of paper ahead of time. Put them in a jar and choose one when you're feeling playful.

CHAPTER 41

⸺◦⟨⟩◦⸺

A Sense of Humor Uplifts the Spirit

Couples who laugh together, stay together.
A well-developed sense of humor
encourages a healthier life.
Laughter releases natural chemicals to
relieve pain, lift spirits, and ease stress.

COUPLES WHO LAUGH TOGETHER, STAY together. You don't need to be a standup comic, able to rattle off one-liner jokes, or consistently display a quick wit. The only thing required is the ability to laugh at the craziness of everyday life. A healthy sense of humor is the type of humor that puts others at ease in embarrassing situations, calms the nerves under stress, and is supportive by putting things in proper perspective.

As years roll by, it becomes easier to forget when you were the young boy with the easy smile or the sweet girl with the soft giggle. To rekindle that spark of innocence, force yourself to find something—anything—that will entice you to laugh. Watch a funny movie or sitcom, listen to your favorite comedian, find an online joke site, attend a comedy show, or check out the funniest animal videos for guaranteed chuckles. Even simpler is to spend time with people who are uplifting to be around. Laughter is contagious!

If you're still having trouble letting go of sadness or problems that are stuck in the subconscious mind, practice mindful laughing by forcing yourself to laugh for several minutes. Adopt the attitude of "fake it until you make it." After you've finished laughing, close your eyes and relax. Feel the lightness integrate within your body. Since your subconscious mind is unable to discriminate between the truth and a lie, it automatically sends the message to your body to release stress. Before you know it, humor has restored your spirit, making any problems more bearable.

The medical community agrees that, when you laugh, smile, and find humor in the mundane, your immune system is strengthened, pain is relieved, and overall health is improved. Whatever improves her mood, uplifts his spirit, or makes her smile, whether exchanging light banter or making jokes to cope with a bizarre situation, having a sense of humor is a gift of love, proving that laughter is still the best medicine.[7]

My mother and father, Evelyn and Ziggie, maintained a true sense of humor throughout serious illnesses, even when things looked most dire. In the waiting room of her chemo treatments, my mom was heard to say, "Why is everyone so depressed? It's only cancer."

---

[7] Beware of the pitfalls of thinking that you should be the life of the party by telling crude stories, poking fun at the less fortunate, or playing practical jokes at someone else's expense. All of these cause embarrassment and may actually deteriorate your relationships.

With each treatment, she enlivened patients with spirited conversation as she canvassed the waiting room and listened to everyone's story. The glow of her positive outlook and childlike attitude stimulated the energy in the waiting room, and the atmosphere became lighter. I'm convinced that her sense of humor was a major factor in her surviving ovarian cancer. When she was joking with her doctor, he said, "Evelyn, you're one of a kind."

My dad was skilled in telling one-liner jokes, and he had one for everyone regardless of occupation—waitresses, nurses, the guy at the deli, and even perfect strangers. He possessed an incredible talent to raise spirits through humor, anytime, anyplace. People who knew him still smile just upon hearing his name. Even when Evelyn would *occasionally* cheat at cards, he would shake his head and laugh. She knew he knew, and he knew she knew that he knew, but it didn't matter. What mattered to them both was that they were having fun. They were playful at whatever they did. Although they have passed on, I'll always remember the lesson of love they shared through their sense of humor.

Jamie shared, "One of the things I love about my husband is the way he jokes me out of my funk. He'll sing some silly song or make some silly comment or tease me, just to make me laugh. He's just one of those amazing people who doesn't sweat the small stuff."

With each chuckle and every belly laugh, your brain releases oxytocin, the so-called love hormone, adding more zing to your day. It stands to reason that, by sharing a sense of humor with your sweetie, uplifting energy is bound to fill your happy home, forever and ever more.

CHAPTER 42

———— •❧•❧• ————

Does Sex Really Matter?

Release your inhibitions, improve your health,
and release natural, pain-relieving "love chemicals."
Making love is more than sex.

"SEX SELLS!" THIS OLD ADAGE has proven true time and time again. As I was writing Mindfully Ever After, one person advised, "If you want to make a lot of book sales, write about sex."

It's true that sometimes it seems that we live in a culture that is obsessed with sex—we encounter it in articles, books, conversations, and TV shows and movies. Pretty much everything in our society has something to do with sex. Although sex does sell, when it comes to true love, does sex really matter?

I'm actually referring to couples who have made a lifelong commitment to one another with an honest, deep emotional connection, to whom making love is so much more than a detached physical act. Lovemaking is magical.

While there's little denying that when "Oh, baby, let me light your fire!" vibrations are sent throughout the body, the entire biological system engages as bodies melt into a one-energy being, exploding with fireworks of love and exponentially enhancing intimacy.

In due course, over time, it's only natural that each couple makes personal decisions of love making activity based on age, health, and circumstances that can, and most likely will, change throughout the years of wedded bliss.

As anniversaries roll by, whether love making is the end goal or not, it's still fun to keep the "izzle" in the sizzle of your love. Whether it's deep long kisses, furtively playing footsie under the dinner table, or meeting in clandestine places—whatever works for you—be mindful to stay connected on the sexual level.

Showing affection doesn't mean that it needs to end with physical interaction. It's simply a matter of letting your mate know that he or she is desirable and is—and always will be—the only one who lights your fire. As one wife said, "I love my husband, and that's that. While I still enjoy making love, as we age, it happens less and less, and I'm okay with that."

Most agree about the value of lovemaking in sharing intimacy, but were you aware that lovemaking releases pain-relieving chemicals? When I was a young and newly married bride, there was a time when I wasn't able to lift my arm. A neurologist diagnosed me with radiculitis, or severe nerve inflammation, that had settled in my upper arm. He said that the nerves would have to heal on their own, and that could take about a year. Meanwhile, rather than advising me to take pharmaceutical medication for the pain, he told me about the brain's natural pain reliever chemicals of dopamine, oxytocin, and serotonin released during love making. Not only was he right about the pain in my arm leaving in a year, he was also right about the benefits of making love for pain relief. I highly recommend it.

In fact, researchers agree that whenever a headache is looming, making love releases the endorphin chemicals which are natural pain relievers. So instead of reaching for the aspirin bottle, try saying, "Honey, I have a headache, so let's make love." Besides a headache, what have you got to lose?

Researchers have found that the art of making love has many health benefits:

- Releases the hormones dopamine, oxytocin, and serotonin, which are natural pain relievers called love chemicals

- Improves the general state of your mental health

- Provides a cardio workout by lowering blood pressure

- Relieves depression[8]

- Liberates chronic headaches

Feeling down? Don't reach for that plate, reach for your mate!

Even if you're going through a dry spell, smile and take a deep breath. You're still getting more affection than if you were single. Keep in mind that making love, like learning to play the piano, improves with practice. And even if it's been a while, remember … you never forget how to ride a bike.

---

[8] Talk to your doctor about the side effects of anti-depression medications.

CHAPTER 43

———◇◆◇———

Sexy Is as Sexy Does

Sexy is in the eyes of the beholder.

"Sexy is as sexy does." Whatever sexy means to you, remember that it's more than what you wear, how you talk, or what you have. Sexy is an attitude that enhances the vivid imagination that is personal to each one of us.

Whether you're thinking dancing poles or black lace stockings, being sexy is in the eye of the beholder. I invite you to join me as I take a stroll down an imaginary road to explore the world of what it means to be sexy:

♥ Sexy is dressing to enhance your assets, like wearing a lacy peek-a-boo bra to reveal a touch of cleavage, angling a well-placed slit to show off lengthy legs, or donning a provocative mini-skirt that carefully leaves something to the imagination.

- ♥ Sexy is being comfortable to show "I like you" while in public. Hold hands, walk arm in arm, offer a spontaneous hug or a gentle kiss.

- ♥ Sexy is being ready for those spur-of the-moment, playful happenings.

- ♥ Sexy is a partner who "gets" you and understands your moods.

- ♥ Sexy is keeping whipped cream on hand when you may need it for more than hot chocolate.

- ♥ Sexy is walking with your head held high and being confident in yourself.

- ♥ Sexy is an attitude that states how comfortable you are in your own skin.

- ♥ Sexy is someone who sets aside special time just for a special someone.

- ♥ Sexy is being equally comfortable in a dive bar or an elegant restaurant.

- ♥ Sexy is a bear hug, a twirl-around hug, or a lingering hug.

- ♥ Sexy is lingerie, silk camis, soft jammies, and lace teddies.

- ♥ Sexy is whispering naughtiness into your lover's ears.

- ♥ Sexy is walking with self-assurance, poise, and posture.

- ♥ Sexy is a soft, gentle voice filled with whispers of love.

- ♥ Sexy is someone who appreciates down-to-earth fun.

♥ Sexy is a knowing wink, a spontaneous kiss.

♥ Sexy is a person who smiles and laughs easily.

♥ Sexy is being sincere, empathetic, and kind.

♥ Sexy is being there when you're needed.

♥ Sexy is having passion for what you do.

♥ Sexy is being able to laugh at yourself.

♥ Sexy is a playful four-letter word.

♥ Sexy is sharing a secret.

♥ Sexy is thoughtfulness.

♥ Sexy is being humble.

♥ Sexy is in the kiss.

♥ Sexy is sharing.

♥ Sexy is wiping away the tears with silent understanding.

♥ Sexy is being authentic to yourself. You are the only you that there is.

Sexy is how you feel about yourself and has absolutely nothing whatsoever to do with sex.

CHAPTER 44

——— ⟨❧⟩ ———

Words to Love By

When searching for words that express your love,
Speak from your heart as lovers do.
Let your words flow as a peaceful dove;
Pen to paper, your love will ring true.

WHETHER WRITTEN OR SPOKEN, WORDS are powerful expressions of everlasting love.

Archaeologists discovered evidence of a love poem inscribed on a clay tablet by a romantic Sumerian around 3500 BC. Words of love also date back to ancient Mesopotamia when marriage was a profitable business; the prettiest women were sold to the wealthiest, the poor guys got the leftovers, and deals were made between the families. Love songs and poems of these unions date as far back as 1750 BC.

It's been said that love makes the world go round. Love also brings out the best of any potential poet. So if there comes a time when you are at a loss for words, here is an alphabetical list of words for you to express your love:

A: apologize, acceptance, admire, adore, adventure, agree, amazing, amour, attentive, awareness, aloha (Hawaiians use this word at meeting and parting. For them it is deeply spiritual and refers to the force that holds us—and the Universe— together.)

B: believe, being, bedazzled, beloved, be your best, blissful, brave, breathtaking, bright, brilliant, beauty

C: calm, captivate, carefree, cheerful, cherish, clarity, comfort, communicate, cooperate, commitment, compassion, compromise, content, conversation, consideration, cosmic, courage, creative, cuddle, cultivate, common sense

D: dazzled, delicate, dedicated, delightful, desire, determined, devoted, divine, don't take it personally

E: empathy, efficient, equality, encouraging, energy, enjoy, enlightened, empowered, exceptional, exciting, eyes, esteem

F: fantastic, fabulous, fascinating, forgive, fair, fun, fondness, friendship

G: gentle, generous, gratitude, giving, grace, graceful, gracious, great, gleeful, goodwill, Godspeed

H: happy, harmony, health, heavenly, helpful, hero, honest, honor, hope, happiness, hug, humility, humor

I: imagine, inspire, independent, intuitive, innocent, intelligent, illuminate, intrigue, infinite, inspire, I love you, interesting, inviting

J: joke around, just for fun, joy, justice

K: kiss every morning, every night, and in between; kindness

L: laugh, loyal, love, lovely, lucky, lustrous

M: magnificent, meditate, mindful, mind-blowing, motivate, mysterious, mine, mahalo (the Hawaiian word for thank you)

N: nature walks, nice, noble, nourish, nurture

O: only you, oh yeah, optimist, open-minded, outstanding

P: patience, passion, peace of mind, perfect, positive, pleasure, peace

Q: quality, quick to laugh, my queen

R: radiate, respect, reciprocate, remarkable, romance, receive

S: sassy, sensual, sincere, smile, sparkle, splendid, spectacular, spunky, spirit, stupendous, support, sweetheart, sweetness, sweetie

T: take responsibility, team, tenderness, thankful, tolerance, thoughtful, trust, true

U: use your skill, understanding, unselfishness, unique

V: value, victory, vocalize your love, valuable, vulnerable

W: will yourself, wishes, worthy, wonderful, wholehearted, wondrous

X: x-citement, xo (hugs and kisses)

Y: yes, dear, you're the best

Z: zany, zest for romance, zeal for love, zen kind of love

Just for fun, pick out a word or phrase every week and see how many times you can work it into your daily conversation and routine. Keep a tally and offer an enticing surprise at the end of the week for the winner.

PART 8
Mindfully in the Now

Living "mindfully in the now" doesn't mean that you need to sit cross-legged, chant, or practice meditation. Being mindful simply means making the choice to live in the present without getting caught up in the confusion of the ego mind. Loving in the present is to love wholly while releasing past patterns and beliefs that no longer serve you.

You are living in the now without even realizing it. There isn't any guarantee what will happen one second from now, so it's impossible to predict the future. Just ask anyone who's been in an accident or had a heart attack. The past has already happened, full of precious life memories safely stored until needed. Live and embrace the now.

To appreciate the present time by sharing your life with someone you love is to acknowledge that, to maintain a healthy and loving relationship, you must practice a heightened sense of awareness. Your togetherness recognizes the need to release conflict and pave the way for the maturity of a deeper love. There are no offensive or defensive strategies where true love is concerned, no games to play. What is required is a surrendering of ego to a field of openness. This allows a space for complete fulfillment and peace of mind.

To be mindfully now, take a deep breath and be fully present in the moment.

CHAPTER 45

———— ·❧·❧· ————

Forever Friends

Friends are supportive, keepers of confidence, and
speakers of truth.
Friends are to be valued.

FOREVER FRIENDS ARE CONTENT TO hear the everyday stuff. They know the good, the bad, and the unspoken desires. No judgment. No criticism.

Friends affirm each other's qualities, enjoy each other's company, and speak the truth, even when she knows that it isn't what he wants to hear. Although he still does bonehead things, friends accept each other unconditionally. Friends know each other's weaknesses and fears and turn to each other for comfort, support, and validation. Despite distractedness during the morning rush and grumpiness at the end of a long day, forever friends love each other.

A friend will always speak of you with respect, regardless of where he is or who's around. Everyone needs to vent a little, and when she does, it's within the confines of a safe environment. A friend doesn't subject her partner to be a topic of gossip or ridicule.

As friends, you may share similar interests, values and philosophies. Friends support each other's hobbies and encourage personal growth. He's dependable, and she knows that he'll never leave her hanging in the lurch. With just one look, she knows exactly what he's saying.

Jim and Gloria were best friends for decades, supporting each other through life's challenges before they figured out that they were meant for each other. His easygoing manner, witty humor, touch of silliness, and total devotion are just a few of the many things Gloria loved about him. "He was my best friend, my rock. We shared absolutely everything! We worked together for years so we already knew that we could get along. He knew everything there was to know about me, and I knew everything about him, so there were never any secrets or surprises. He understood me, you know? He made me laugh, and I'll always love him."

Friends share their deepest secrets and loftiest dreams, knowing that they're in safe keeping. She'll let you know that you're loved and will always have your best interest at heart. He remembers that it's the little things that count.

As one wife said, "My husband and I love each other unconditionally. He's passionate. He's romantic. He's really too good to be true. Sometimes I have to remind myself not to take him for granted."

The best vitamin to take if you want your partner as a friend is to B-1.

CHAPTER 46

Rejuvenate!

Be mindful of the three Rs:
Renew your love,
Reacquaint your heart with passion,
Reconnect with your spirit as one.

ALL WORK AND NO PLAY makes Tarzan and Jane dull and weary. When your response to snuggling or getting nookie is "I'm just too damn tired," it's time to follow the three Rs of relationships: renew, reacquaint, and reconnect. The moment you begin to make plans to get away from everyday stress, the neurotransmitters in the brain say "Yippee!" and send an energy boost of dopamine happiness.

To prepare for the three Rs of rejuvenation, first design a plan. Check your calendar, pick up the phone and schedule a mini vacation. Whether you check into a luxurious hotel, drive to a cabin in the mountains, or fly to an exotic island--- just do it!

Whatever your budget, brain storm and explore alternatives. Set your creative juices into motion and come up with something unique. Once positive intention is stated, be prepared to be amazed how it will all come together---just do it!

It doesn't matter how old you are or how long you've been married, a change of environment offers new experiences and is bound to boost your relationship.

To rejuvenate a relationship:

- Renew your love by holding hands. Stare into each other's eyes. Admire the moonlight and stars. Watch a sunset and be in awe together.

- Reacquaint yourselves with your dreams. Reminisce about how you met and fell in love. Remember what it was like when you touched each other for the first time.

- Reconnect by keeping the excitement alive. Role-playing is a fun way to discover new interests, thoughts, and updates about each other.

Whatever you choose, agree to leave all work and computers at home. Turn off the cell phones.

Begin with a thought, set the intention to create uninterrupted time together, and it *will* happen. Whether your rejuvenation get-away is an occasional weekend, every weekend, or a yearly vacation, set a date and put the process in motion. Trust all will fall neatly into place. Renew. Reacquaint. Reconnect.

CHAPTER 47

·❦·

Interests

Discover new interests to nurture togetherness.

INDIVIDUAL HOBBIES HELP YOU TO stay true to yourself. Additionally, they provide a healthy space in your togetherness. However, by exploring and discovering fresh interests to explore together, you'll actively be keeping the liveliness in your marriage.

There are many common interests for couples to delve into, like cooking, hiking, and gardening. You can come up with hundreds more. On your search for an interest that neither of you has experienced before, expect that there will be activities that are certain to be written off completely, while something else may score as a perfect fit. Regardless of what you decide, you'll be building a memory bank of stories to tell—the huge fish that got away, how you trained for a marathon, or the secret to the perfect soufflé.

Whatever interest you decide on, be mindful to stay open minded and maintain a positive attitude. Release preconceived notions and explore whatever you choose with full abandon. While your phone's SD card is being filled with photo memories, your "remember when we ..." memories will be even better exaggerated as time goes on.

Meanwhile, if you currently have similar interests you equally share, bravo! Just tuck this thought in your back pocket whenever your sweetie says there's nothing to do.

Of course, common sense must prevail. Don't attempt anything dangerous to your health or well-being, so activities like tightrope walking, crocodile wrestling, and running with the bulls might be a no-go. Other considerations that must be taken into consideration include your age, physical abilities, and any health issues.

CHAPTER 48

———— ·❧❧· ————

To Sleep or Not to Sleep?

Don't go to bed without saying "I love you."
Clear your mind and energy for the next day.
Take deep breaths, meditate, or play
soothing music to calm anxiety.

TO SLEEP OR NOT TO sleep, that is the question. "Don't go to bed angry" is advice that has been offered at every bridal shower I've ever attended. And I've been to a lot of bridal showers!

Kissing, making up, and saying "I love you" before your head hits the pillow is solid advice. This practice releases toxic energy, and it makes perfect sense to begin the next morning with a fresh, clear mind, welcoming a new sunrise.

The original reason behind the standard rule of not going to bed angry was based on the theory that going to bed with unresolved issues meant that the unsettled argument would become imbedded in the subconscious mind. Once in the subconscious, it would stew at a slow-cooker simmer, erupting at a later date, like the infamous straw that broke the camel's back.

How does one determine which arguments need to be resolved before going to sleep and which ones can wait to be rescheduled? Consider putting everyday human errors in the proper perspective by realizing the significance of things in the bigger picture of life. Current thinking is that there are circumstances when it's okay to go to bed without reaching a resolution:

- Have you ever tried reasoning with someone who's had too much alcohol? Not only is it a waste of time, the argument could escalate and get ugly. Save your energy, let him or her sleep it off, and talk in the morning. Hopefully, over indulgence isn't a frequent occurrence. If it is, there are more significant issues that need to be addressed.

- What if you have to get up really early the next day and need to be on alert? Whether you're a butcher, baker, or candlestick maker, whatever job you have, being rested is crucial for you to do your best and stay safe while doing it. Speaking of safe, if you're driving the next morning, without proper rest, you'll be putting yourself and others in danger.

- What point is there in rehashing the same old argument over and over with no end in sight? Go to bed. With a clear head, you may see things differently in the morning. This requires self-control to understand that repeating the same argument is like a toy train going round and round in circles, huffing and puffing, but going nowhere. If this argument involves breaking boundaries, finances, or in-laws, it's most likely time to seek objective professional help.

- Sometimes, one thing leads to another, and before you know it, the original argument is lost and you've completely been derailed.

Her: "How could you have forgotten to let the dog in?"

Him: "I was on the computer and lost track of time."

Her: "That's another thing, you and that damn computer!"

Him: "Me? At least I'm not ordering fifty things a day from online stores!"

At times like this, take a breather, go to bed and reset your emotional inner system. There's obviously more going on than bringing the dog in. What is the real issue here? a) I've had a long day. b) I'm exhausted. c) I'm not feeling well. d) The boss yelled at me. e) I just need to sleep. f) It's your dog, not mine. g) You like the dog more than you like me. h) Whatever. If you're too tired, then you're too tired. Just don't use this as an excuse for avoiding the heart of the issue indefinitely.

Make sure to follow up with real communication by setting a definite day and time to resume the conversation. Stick to finding a resolution before avoidance turns into resentment.

Current thinking is that it's okay to go to bed to "sleep on it" as long as you reschedule and reach resolution. You can still be miffed, but a good-night kiss and saying "I love you" will give both of you a solid night's rest. In the morning, you'll both be rested and better able to restart the conflict or decide on a more suitable time.

What if you've kissed and said "I love you" but your mind is racing as each word replays in your head, and your insides are still jumbled from anger. How can you possibly calm yourself?

To tranquilize the adrenaline rush, write down your feelings and concerns. Keep paper and pencil on your nightstand. If you wake up with a new angle to add to your perspective, rather than dwell on it, write your thoughts down and let them go. In the morning, you can read your notes with a clear mind. You'll either say to yourself, "I truly am a genius! Why didn't I think of this sooner?" Or you may say "What the hell was I thinking? I sound like a complete dolt!"

There are other ways to calm what's called a "monkey mind": take deep breaths, meditate, or play relaxing music. Stay in the attitude of being in the grace of gratitude, and count your blessings instead of complaints.

One wife said, "We used to argue well into the night. It got to the point where I had to stop or I'd never get a good night's sleep. We just decided not to talk about certain subjects anymore. I respect his point of view, and he respects mine. That's all there is to it."

For those of you who still believe in staying awake until an argument is resolved, at least set an alarm or timer. If a resolution isn't found before the agreed-upon time, when the alarm dings, agree to disagree and reschedule. Things are bound to look better in the morning.

Bottom line: Sleep deprivation helps no one.

New rule: Don't go to bed without saying "I love you."

CHAPTER 49

———— ·❊·❊· ————

Space in Your Togetherness

Create space in your togetherness.
Personal space enhances self-growth
and maintains independence.
Meet up in the middle as a couple.

EVERYONE NEEDS SPACE. YES, YOU'RE a couple, yet you're still individuals with separate thoughts. Even though you love spending time with your other half, do you find yourself still desiring space for personal growth? What do you do or where do you go when you need to gain clarity of thought or search within? Whatever your dreams, creating space in your relationship is a valuable commodity.

One husband converted a garage into an oasis of peace as his personal retreat. His wife understands and gives him the space he needs. When I asked him what makes his marriage last, he shrugged his shoulders and said, "I don't know." He laughed. "Whatever it is seems to work. Guess we just really like each other."

While honoring your own pursuits, it's important to remember that your partner needs space, too. Like a pair of pants, you may be joined at the waist as one, but as the physical body demands, each leg needs its own space. When you trust and have faith in your partner and support the need for space in your togetherness, then you'll evolve stronger than ever as a couple. It's in the nature of the soul to do what the soul needs to do in order to grow.

Jamie needed two hundred teaching hours to become a certified yoga instructor. Realizing that if she spent a few hours here and there, it would take years to meet her goal, she found a month-long program with only one catch—it was out of the country. When I asked her what her husband, Adam, thought about it, she explained that they had written a list of pros and cons before making a decision. She now says, "I have an amazing husband! Thanks to his total support, I am now a certified yoga instructor."

As a talented artist, one wife explains how she and her husband show support: "My husband doesn't paint, but he supports me every time he goes to one of my art shows." How does she support him in return? "Well, he's a fisherman, so I support him by buying fish at the grocery store and cooking him a delicious fish dinner, which he especially appreciates when he comes home empty handed."

To honor space takes cooperation to manage and adjust work schedules around the job, kids, and family obligations with full appreciation of your partner.

What do you do if you have a partner who considers your hobby and/or goals irrelevant? Once energy is drained, intimacy becomes strained, and resentment takes its place. Before that happens, have matter-of-fact dialogue to speak your truth. If the problem continues, seek professional help. If you're the one fearful of letting go of control, take time to do some serious self-reflection.

Always remember to meet in the middle. Whether over a cup of morning coffee or a leisurely glass of wine after work, together time still has priority.

PART 9

Mindful Beliefs

Research by major universities confirms that increasing "mindfulness" benefits young and old alike. Mindfulness heightens the ability to calm the "monkey mind," increase body awareness, and psychologically improve the level of compassion and empathy while reducing anxiety and depression.

Although the practice of being mindful is thousands of years old, in the twenty-first century, more mindfulness training programs are thankfully being created to teach techniques for building and maintaining healthy relationships.

CHAPTER 50

·⟨3⋅⟨3⟩·

Where Faith Resides

Honor and respect each other's spiritual beliefs.
Continue to grow in faith, forgiveness,
and unconditional love.

THE PLACE IN YOUR HEART where faith resides is like a well-built home; it is strong enough to withstand any challenge or storm, yet tender and flexible, filled with compassion and kindness. The spiritual framework of any home has many rooms. One is filled with hope, another with respect; still others are filled with trust, love, and a sense of living in the grace of God. A home where faith resides is one of care and guidance, comfort in knowing you are exactly where you're meant to be.

Barbara describes how faith plays a role in her silver-anniversary marriage: "I think that what keeps marriages together is faith in God and spending time together. God teaches us love, forgiveness, and self-sacrifice. Believing in God and His teachings makes us accountable to God. He is our reason for working hard to resolve our issues and staying together. Spending time together is essential to a marriage. A couple's time together is a growing time, a bonding and binding time. As we consistently spend time together, we become intertwined, and the two do become one!"

Weaving together a family unit able to endure life's battles requires a well-defined code of ethics and unshakable values that are woven early into the marriage. These values will persevere through any trouble that crosses your path. You have spoken marriage vows to bind you both together. To build a home where faith resides, use "promise" as the cement between the bricks to secure and bond your love regardless of outside influences of winds or storms.

Once two souls are joined in a sacred ceremony, whether in a courthouse, a church, or under the stars, there is an assumed understanding that building a unified family begins with "I do."

If you should ever decide to have children, it's even more vital to discuss what spiritual practices you expect to have honored. Whether you decide to follow family religious practices or start fresh by seeking a church or spiritual group with like-minded people, have the discussion now, so, should the day ever come, the cement has already been poured and set.

Through compassion, tolerance and respect of each other's beliefs, marriage is strengthened and destined to thrive. You and your partner have committed to the same dance of life, as individuals *and* as a couple. As years pass, unavoidable challenges will cross your path filled with life lessons to learn. You'll also have bonding moments of opportunities, growth, and experiences to share, building a stockpile of memories.

Bee (Debbee) describes herself as a spiritual person and attends a spiritualist church. Mike, her husband of eighteen years, is devoutly religious and regularly attends a Catholic church. Bee says "When the weather is nasty and the roads questionable, Mike attends an earlier mass just so he can be home in time to drive me to service and drop me off at the front entrance of my church. Then he patiently waits for me until the service is over to drive me home. Whenever there's a special occasion at his church, I'm happy to go. We deeply respect each other. Never, ever would either of us make any kind of disparaging remark about each other's religious beliefs. I would never try to change him, and he would never try to change me. I feel as if I hit the lottery with him!"

With united faith in your love, you're well equipped to conquer any adversities. Your values and your beliefs in one another are the hammer and nail that unify your marriage. Through your jointure as one, you're certain to prevail over the fleeting flight of time standing together in divine light.

CHAPTER 51

—⟨3•8⟩—

The Circle of Love

Wedding bands are symbols of everlasting love.
Wear your wedding ring as a sign of commitment.

THE WEDDING RING IS A symbol that represents everlasting love because it has no beginning and no end. Wearing a wedding ring is a sign of commitment that silently states to the world, "My heart belongs to another." The circle of metal that embraces your finger embodies the sharing of a life's journey between two special people who managed to find each other in a sea of millions.

Although the exact year isn't known, most historians agree that the history of wearing wedding rings dates back six thousand years ago to the ancient Egyptians. The Egyptians braided rings out of fibers from the papyrus plant. When the rings eventually wore out, they would create new ones of leather, bone, or ivory. When metallurgy was discovered, metals were used, and eventually precious gems were added. The hole in the center of the ring represented an opening to a gateway shared into unknown worlds.

It is customary to wear the wedding ring on the fourth finger of the left hand. This began with the belief that the vein of this finger, the *vena amoris* or the vein of love, led directly to the heart. Although this isn't true, the custom remains. However, in several countries, such as Greece and Germany, the wedding ring is worn on the right hand.

Women were once the only receivers of wedding rings, but in the 1930s, rings for men were introduced in America. As soldiers went off to World War Two, women began giving their husbands wedding rings to wear as reassuring reminders that there were loved ones waiting for them back home as they went overseas. By the late 1940s in America, 80 percent of weddings were double-ring ceremonies.

As the ring represents lifelong love, should your ring ever become lost, replace it after a reasonable amount of time, even if you can't afford one as expensive as the original. To make the replacement ring as unique and sentimental as possible as the first one, be sure to create a special ceremony, even if it's just between the two of you. Whether you share a romantic ambiance under the stars or in front of a warm fireplace on a frosty night, find a special place where you can restate your vows by recommitting your love to one another.

There are a few exceptions to wearing a ring 24/7. Some people have allergies to various kinds of metal. Others work at jobs where wearing a ring could create a potential injury, such as working around machinery. There may be other circumstances in which wearing a ring could cause danger to yourself or others. In some cases, precious metals could be damaged through exposure to on-the-job processes. Also, it might be wise to leave your rings at home if you are going to be doing something like boating or skiing or if you are going to be wearing gardening or work gloves. It would be easy to lose your ring in these circumstances. Common sense must prevail.

Most of the time, wear your wedding ring with pride as a commitment to your love.

CHAPTER 52

———— ❖ ————

The Will to Love

Will yourself to stay in love.
You will be amazed what a little
"spiritual will" power can do.

"WHERE THERE'S A WILL, THERE'S a way." Imagine a child pulling a chair to the counter to raid the cookie jar. Regardless of how high the jar is placed, he's determined to get the cookie. So it is with your "will to love."

The "will" referred to in this context of love is a spiritual will. Your spiritual will resides deep within your soul and possesses an unshakable conviction of faith that your marriage will be a lasting one. Spiritual will is not a thought in the mind; rather, it is the light contained within the heart of your spirit. When you will yourself to love, you possess a belief that, no matter what problems come your way, whatever mood you happen to be in, or whatever other people say or do, your love will remain as infinite as the cosmos.

Through mindfulness, you have the ability to program your conscious mind with positive thoughts. While the subconscious mind follows your daily living instincts, your conscious mind creates beneficial behaviors and thoughts to enhance your life. Once spiritual will is integrated into the subconscious mind, it becomes as second nature as putting one foot in front of the other.

Most people have been conditioned since childhood to react in certain ways. So, when you have the desire to react differently, in a more positive way, you need to reprogram your subconscious mind through conscious-mind thinking. Whenever you feel eager to do something you know isn't in your best interest, take control of your conscious mind and tell it no! By taking control of your thoughts, you'll be able to live your life in the most positive way possible.

At times, for whatever reason, you may find yourself annoyed with your spouse. In a split second, you may think, *I just want to be left alone.* You may even think about saying something unkind in that moment. This is when your spiritual will—or your will to love—must kick into gear. In that nanosecond, you pause to realize that you love this person, this person whom you find to be totally annoying. Even though you want to be left alone, in your heart of hearts, you know how much your love abides, even with all the quirks and annoying habits.

As you look at your mate through loving eyes, rewind the tape in your memory bank by playing back all the times you've welcomed the tender smack on the behind and nuzzle on your neck. As memories of love surface, your heart begins to swell once again, saying, "Thank you, God, for bringing this amazing person into my life."

Powerful emotions begin with a spark in the heart. Whenever you listen to the unconscious voice of the heart, love will triumph. Your will to love is instantly available whenever it's needed.

To check your spiritual will, ask yourself a few simple questions:

- Have you ever willed yourself to do something that you really didn't want to do simply because she said "pretty please"?

- Have you ever gone someplace that you really didn't want to go because you knew how important it was to him?

- Have you ever compromised because you knew it meant more to her than to you?

If you've done all this and more, then your spiritual will sounds like it's just fine.

A Minister Explains His Spiritual Will

As my mother's elderly minister was scheduled to visit her in the hospital, I asked her if she thought he would mind if I interviewed him about marriage. She laughed. "I already did! He said that would be fine." When he arrived, he was prepped when I started by asking, "How long have you been married?"

"Sixty years," he said with a satisfied smile as I jotted it down.

Then I asked, "What can you tell me about a healthy marriage that I haven't already heard?"

Pastor was deep in thought for several minutes. My mom and I sat in solemn silence, patiently waiting for his words of wisdom: "My wife is a very loving, happy person, especially in the morning." He paused, searching for the right words. "On many mornings she greets me with a kiss and a sing-song, joyful 'Good morning!' when all I really want is to be left alone. But then I think about how much I love her and how important a kiss is to her, so I go ahead and let her kiss me, and I kiss her back. Pretty soon, she has me talking and feeling happy. I'm glad that she does that. If she left me alone, or if I asked her to leave me alone,

---

I don't know if I would feel the same throughout the day. So, I guess my answer would be that I *will* myself to stay in love. I *will* myself to hug her and kiss her even when I don't want to. After all, I chose her, and she chose me. That's probably one of the biggest reasons we've been together for so long."

Although the pastor and his wife have passed away, I'll wager that they've *willed* themselves to be together in spirit.

Whenever you're feeling that tug of annoyance, be sure to check in with your spiritual will before you react by saying or doing something you'll later regret, and always remember to will yourself to love.

You were born together, and together you shall be forevermore.

You shall be together when the white wings
of death scatter your days.

Ay, you shall be together even in the silent memory of God.

But let there be spaces in your togetherness,

And let the winds of the heavens dance between you.

Kahlil Gibran

GRATITUDES

I AM FOREVER GRATEFUL FOR the love and encouragement of my family and friends. Their gifts of wisdom and realistic insights added a personal touch of encouragement to the birth of this book.

I offer special gratitude to all who contributed in any way on how to follow the path to wedded bliss: Aline, Barbara, Bee, Betty, Bonnie, Caryl, Camille, Eva and David, Gloria, Jean and Fred, Joan, Joanne and Hank, Chris and Jeff, Jamie and Adam, Judy, Julie, Linda, Melissa, Nancy, Neil and Nicole, Norine, Rose, Stacey and Mike, Walter. You have all been an inspiration to forever after love.

Grateful thanks to my sister-in-law, Eva Montealegre, for having the imaginative vision to create the elegant cover design.

Grateful thanks to my brother, DJ Zelczak, for his creativity in writing the unique heartfelt love poem "Wedding Vows."

Were it not for the work of researchers and the institutions for which they work, and their many studies that provided insight into successful relationships, there would be no book. Thank you. Keep up the great work.

I am eternally grateful to my parents: To my dad for his indomitable strength of character, who taught me lifelong lessons through stories, humor, and love. To my mom who danced as if no one was watching, teaching me to be true to myself.

Gratitude always to my beloved children, Jamie and Neil, who have blessed me with the gift of motherhood. They have been my inspiration and anchor.

Thank you to the people at Balboa Press: The entire editorial department---Jan, for her thoughtful suggestions and comments, Hannah, for her kind encouragement and Michael for his patience to guide me through the publishing process.

I am grateful for you, mindful readers. May this book be a reminder that *love* is the most powerful vibration on earth, and, like the mustard seed, can grow into a formidable force.

May you always live in the grace and gratitude of love.

Dearest Readers,

As I prepare to send Mindfully Ever After to the publisher, the coronavirus—or COVID-19—pandemic is in full swing. The feeling is surreal as stores and restaurants are closed to minimize physical contact in order to "flatten the curve." Weddings in large venues are postponed, and some couples are opting to marry at the local chapel. Honeymoons, vacations, and sporting events like March Madness have been canceled. The world as I knew it yesterday has changed. Hand sanitizer and wipes are scarce, and toilet paper is more precious than silver!

Here in Pittsburgh, and throughout the nation, and world, theaters, concerts, and fundraisers are at a standstill. There are no family gatherings or lunches with friends. No more shaking hands, hugging, or tailgate parties. Technology has become the main source of communicating. Sunday church services are often offered via the internet.

The entire community of the world is affected. This germ inhabits and destroys indiscriminately, although the elderly seem to be more vulnerable. The danger is that transmission from person to person is incredibly high and people can have the virus and be unsuspecting carriers. "Social distancing" is the watchword of the day. The wearing of masks is commonplace, and usually mandatory.

How are couples handling this pandemic? Many are out of work, others are working under stressful conditions, and the lucky ones are able to work from home. It's a tremendous financial concern adding emotional strain and stress on countless families.

After days of binge-watching movies, families are becoming reacquainted by reading, playing games, taking walks, and praying. Couples are adjusting and finding new routines to cope.

When you tell your grandkids about the pandemic of 2020, remember and share how you were affected. You can tell them how patience, tolerance, and common-sense behaviors offered hope to restore order to the natural world. You can teach them about how people came together to remind us what's important in life: human kindness for each other.

Just as my children had a "new normal" after 9/11 with upgraded security at airports and gatherings, so shall my grandchildren now have a new normal with a new understanding of the act of touching and knowledge of the fragility of life. History will remember how we handled this transformation of events. It is my deepest hope that historians are able to report that we were kind to one another.

I hope and pray that you have heeded the warnings and have taken all the necessary precautions to stay safe. Watch out for one another and be mindful in your love. May you live your life in joy, grace and gratitude. Each moment counts.

In mindfulness,

Paulette

REFERENCES

Ackerman, Joshua M., Griskevicius, Vladas, and Li, Norman P. (2011). "Let's Get Serious; Communicating Commitment in Romantic Relationships." *Journal of Personality and Social Psychology.* 100 (6), 1079-1094. June 2011. Psycnet.apa.org.

Arnold, Elliott. 1979. *Blood Brother.* New York: University of Nebraska Press. https://nebraskapress.uni.edu.

Alicke, M. D., and Zell, E. (2009). "Social Attractiveness and Blame." *Journal of Applied Social Psychology,* 39, 2089-2105.

Bandler, Richard, and John Grinder. 1979. *Frogs into Princes: Neuro Linguistic Programming.* Real People Press.

Bellows, Amy. 2013. "Good Communication in Marriage Starts with Respect." Psych Control. January, 2013.

Benjamin, Felissa and medically reviewed by Samuel Mackenzie. 2019. "Does Sex Ease Migraine Attacks or Trigger Them?" Everyday Health. July, 2019. everydayhealth.com.

Bennett, H. J. 2003. "Humor in Medicine." *Southern Medical Journal* 96: 1257–1261.

Beris, Rebecca. December, 2016. "5 Things That Will Happen to Your Brain When You Dance." Women's Brain Health Initiative. womensbrainhealth.org.

Berman, Laura. 2011. *Loving Sex: The Book of Joy and Passion*. DK. (July 2011).

Bethune, Sophie. 2015. "Money Stress weighs on Americans' health." American Psychological Association. (April 2015) Vol 46, No. 4. apa.org.

Billups, Tammy. 2018. "How Emotions Manifest in Your Body." *Conscious Life Journal*, January, 2018.

Black, Gary. History of Wedding Rings. 2020. Lifehopeandtruth.com.

Blum, J. S., and A. Mehrabian. 1999. "Personality and Temperament Correlates of Marital Satisfaction." *Journal of Personality* 67: 93–125.

Brown, Brené. 2012. "How Vulnerability Holds the Key to Emotional Intimacy." *Spirituality & Health*, November–December 2012.

Brugman, Delenee. *Happily Wed and Happily Fed*. iUniverse: September, 2009.

Bryant, Ben. 2011. "Judges are more lenient after taking a break, study finds." *The Guardian*, April, 2011.

Caldwell, Miriam and James, Margaret. 2020. "When Your Spouse Won't Participate in a Financial Plan or Budget." The Balance. Updated July 25, 2020. www.thebalance.com.

Currie, Dave. 2010. "Marriage: What Kissing Does for Your Marriage." June 14, 2010. doingfamilyright.com.

Davis, Daphne M., and Jeffery A. Hayes. 2011. "What Are the Benefits of Mindfulness? A Practice Review of Psychotherapy-Related Research." *Psychotherapy* 48, no. 2 (2011): 198–208.

Dobson, Roger. 1999. "Health: The dark side of the mood." *The Independent Culture*, April, 1999.

Dvorsky, George. 2012. "10 Reasons Why Oxytocin is the Most Amazing Molecule in the World." July, 2012.

Emery, Léa Rose. 2019. "Is Your Phone Ruining Your Relationship?" *Brides*, May 31, 2019.

Falk, Leah. 2016. "The Fakelore of the Apache Wedding Blessing." The Awl. February 11, 2016. https://www.theawl.com/2016/02/the-fakelore-of-the-apache-wedding-blessing/.

Financial Industry Regulatory Authority. Finra.org. 2019.

Fisher, Helen. 2004. *Why We Love*. New York: Holt.

Fisher, Roger, and William Ury. 1983. *Getting to Yes: Negotiating Agreement Without Giving In*. London: Penguin Books.

Fulbright, Yvonne K. 2014. "Mate, Rebate and Communicate." December 30, 2014.

GCF Global Learning. "Constructing I-Statements." http://www.gcflearnfree.org. 2019.

Gibran, Kahlil. 1923. *The Prophet*. New York: Alfred A. Knopf.

Glassman, Barry. "4 Things John Oliver Got Right On Investing (And the Big Item He Missed). *Forbes*. June 23, 2016. Forbes.com.

Gottman, John, and Nan Silver. 2000. *The Seven Principles for Making Marriage Work*. Great Britain: Orion Books.

Guinness World Records Limited. February, 2019. "Oldest Love Poem." guinnessworldrecords.com

Harding, Brett. 2016. "How Important is Kissing in a Relationship?" Huffingtonpost.co.uk. June 7, 2016.

Hellman, Rick. 2017. "Relationship success tied not to joking but shared sense of humor." February 8, 2017. News.ku.edu.

Heitler, Susan. 1997. *The Power of Two: Secrets to a Strong and Loving Marriage*. New Harbinger Publications. May, 1997.

Hrala, Josh. July 1, 2016. Science Alert. *People who Meditate Appear to Be More Aware of Their Unconscious Mind*. sciencealert.com.

Hutchinson, John, and Nancy Hutchinson. 2010. "528HZ sound Miraculously Cleaned Oil Polluted Water in the Guld Of Mexico, According to a New Study By A Canadian Researcher." 528records.com

Jankowiak, Karol. 2014. "The Love Frequency 528 HZ." Waking Times. February 5, 2014. Wakingtimes.com.

Jantz, Gregory L., and Ann McMurray. 2009. *Healing the Scars of Emotional Abuse*. Revell (February, 2009)

Jones, Jeffery M. 2016. "Majority in U.S. Do Not Have a Will." Gallup. May 18, 2016. News.gallup.com.

Kirschner, Diane. 2009. "The Shocking State of Marriage: Survey results." *Psychology Today* June 18, 2009. PsychologyToday.com.

Koenig, H. G., M. E. McCollough, and D. B. Larson, eds. 2001. *Handbook of Religion and Health.* New York: Oxford University Press. (1998).

Lee, Harper. *To Kill A Mockingbird.* Harper Perennial Modern. (January, 2002).

Lerner, Harriet. 2012. *Marriage Rules: A Manual for the Married and the Coupled Up.* Avery Publishing Group. (December, 2012).

Light, Kathleen C. 2007. *NIH News in Health.* Hugs. Research University of North Carolina at Chapel Hill. (2007).

Logan, Marilyn. 2006. *I Can't Afford to Marry You.* Houston: Salo Publishing. (January, 2006).

Lore, Diane. "Fight Fair and Keep the Peace in your Relationship." WebMD. 2018.

Loren, Mark. 2003. "The Effects of Religious Beliefs in Marriage and Family." *Marriage and Families.* (August 2003).

Luscombe, Belinda. 2008. "The Science of Romance: Why We Flirt." *Time.* January 17, 2008.

Lusinski, Natalia. 2018. "7 Ways Arguing Benefits Your Relationship, According to Experts." Bustle. February 22, 2018.

Luskin, Fred. 2002. *Forgive for Good: A Proven Prescription for Health and Happiness.* New York: Harper Collins Publishers.

Luskin, Fred, and Kenneth R. Pelletier. 2005. *Stress Free for Good.* New York: Harper Collins Publishers.

Lyons, Linda. 2005. "Last Wishes: Half of Americans Have Written Wills: Most don't have living wills." June 7, 2005. News.gallup.com

Mark, Joshua J. 2014. "Love, Sex, and Marriage in Ancient Mesopotamia." Ancient History Encyclopedia. May 16, 2014.

Mayo Clinic Staff. 2016. "Stress relief from Laughter? It's no joke." Mayo Clinic. April 21, 2016.

Mehrabian, A. (1972). Non verbal Communication. Aldine-Atherton.

Mehrabian, Albert, and Susan R. Ferris. 1967. *Communication: importance of verbal and non-verbal messages.*

McGraw, Phil. 2015. "How to Fight Fair / My Mother-In-Law Drives Me Crazy." www.drphil.com/advice/my-mother-in-law-drives-me-crazy.

McNulty, James K. 2010. *Current Directions in Psychological Science* 19, no. 3 (June 2010): 167–171.

Myss, Caroline. 1997. *Why People Don't Heal; and How They Can.* New York: Harmony Books.

Nicastro, Richard. 2010. *Relationship Help: Patience is a Marital Virtue.* Las Cruces, NM.

Oliver, John. "Retirement Plans: Last Week Tonight with John Oliver." You Tube. June 12, 2016.

Orman, Suze. 2015. PBS broadcast. January 27, 2015.

Pease, Allen. *The Body Language of Love.* Center for Non-verbal Studies. 2012. Orion Publishing Co.

Palmer, Scott, and Bethany Palmer. 2013. *The 5 Money Personalities: Speaking the Same Love and Money Language.* Nashville: Thomas Nelson.

Pines, A. M., and C. F. Bowes. 1992. "Romantic Jealousy: How to recognize where jealousy comes from and how to cope with it." *Psychology Today,* March 1992.

Price, Deborah L. 2012. *The Heart of Money: A Couple's Guide to Creating True Financial Intimacy.* Novato, CA: New World Library.

Pritchard, Justin. 2019. "Are Credit Unions a Safe Place for Your Money?" February 23, 2019. Thebalance.com.

Quilliam, Susan. 1997. *Body Language Secrets.* Harper Collins Publishers.

Rahim, Lucy. 2017. "What to do if you argue before bed." *Lifestyle Women,* January 11, 2017.

Ramsey, David. Financial Advisor, Radio talk host. 2015.

Rich, Jonathan. 2003. *The Couples Guide to Love and Money.* Harbinger Publications. February, 2003.

Richards, Chip. 2016. "What are the Six Basic Human Needs?" chiprichards.global.

Robinson, Kara Mayer. "10 Surprising Health Benefits of Sex." WebMD. October, 2013.

Robinson, L. C., and P. W. Blanton. 1993. "Marital Strengths in Enduring Marriages." *Family Relations* 42 (1993): 38–45.

Robinson, L. C. 1994. "Religious orientation in enduring marriages: An exploratory study." *Review of Religious Research* 35 (1994): 207–218.

Rubin, Lucy. 2017. *The Telegraph. Lifestyle Women.* January, 2017.

Ruiz, Don Miguel. 1997. *The Four Agreements: A Personal Guide to Personal Freedom.* San Rafael, CA: Amber-Allen Publishing.

Rushlow, Amy, and Melissa Matthews. 2018. "How Many Calories Do You Burn During Sex?" *Men's Health,* June 1, 2018.

"Good Luck and Godspeed." 1999. *Scientific American,* July 19, 1999.

Scott, Elizabeth. "The Importance of Vacations for Stress Relief." *Production and Health,* June 1, 2014.

Sinrich, Jenn. 2019. "What Your Social Media Posts Say About Your Relationship." *Brides,* September 2019.

Tessina, Tina B. *Love Styles: How to Celebrate Your Differences.* CreateSpace Independent Publishing Platform, August, 2011.

Tipping, Colin. 2014. *25 Practical Uses for Radical Forgiveness.* Marietta, GA: Global Publications.

Tolle, Eckhart. 1999. *The Power of NOW.* Vancouver, BC: Namaste Publishing.

Wikipedia. Wedding ring history. References: Oliver, Juliet. Retrieved September 9, 2014.

Weisser, Cybele. 2014. "7 Ways to Stop Fighting About Money and Grow Richer, Together." *Money,* June, 2014.

Whipple, Robert. 5 C's of Body Language. 2011. Changingminds.org.

Wilcox, W. Bradford. *The National Marriage Project.* University of Virginia. http://www.stateofourunions.org December 2010.

Wile, Daniel B. 1988. *After the Honeymoon: How Conflict Can Improve Your Relationship*. Canada: John Wiley and Sons.

Williams, Kipling D. 2002. *Ostracism: The Power of Silence*. New York: The Guilford Press. July, 2002.

Wong, Brittany. 2018. *What It Means When Couples Constantly Post About Each Other On Social Media*. February, 2018. Huffpost.com

Zak, Paul. 2012. *The Moral Molecule*. Dutton Publishing.